Praise for *The Crea*

"This book combines Amantha's knowledge of science, psychology and creativity in a fun, useful and practical way. If you want to get your creative juices flowing or that of your team then I couldn't recommend it more highly."
— **Peter Williams, CEO, Deloitte Digital**

"Amantha's book makes the sometimes-esoteric nature of creativity tangible for anyone. Supported by scientific study and easy-to-follow examples, this book can help both individuals and organisations inject the spark of creativity into their world and unearth great ideas."
— **Lee Hunter, product marketing manager, Google**

"In plain English, with great verve, Amantha Imber translates hundreds of psychological studies into workable tactics for awakening creativity. If you catch some of your friends squeezing an object with their hand (won't tell you which one!) before an important meeting, you know they've read Amantha Imber's marvellous book. It has forty-nine further practical, scientifically established strategies for making all of us as creative as we dream of being, all imparted in a real fun way, and easy to apply."
— **Professor Roald Hoffmann, Nobel prize-winning chemist and writer, Cornell University**

"As a person on a journey to greater creativity, and also as part of a company on a similar journey, I loved this book. It offers easy to read, easy to understand and easy to implement tips and ideas to make life more creative and much more fun. Unlike many other books on this subject it is presented in bite-sized chunks to make it more practical, and is based on interesting scientific studies, which can be used to combat the cynicism of the less creative thinkers in our lives."
— **Linda Watts, general manager-strategic innovation, Kimberly Clark South Asia**

"This book is a very refreshing blend of the scientific, the practical and the creative. Any book about creativity that encourages me to sit in a messy, yellow office, play video games, and imagine having dinner with Angelina Jolie, gets my vote."
— **Guy Murphy, worldwide planning director, JWT**

"My company has used Amantha to facilitate numerous creative sessions where I have seen a number of the ideas she has shared in her book in practice. Suffice to say we have generated 100s of creative ideas with people that wouldn't call themselves creative types. The ideas are easy to implement, don't cost a fortune and are lots of fun. I am looking forward to working my way through the fifty ideas she shares in her book to foster further creative thought within the business."
— **Amanda Woollard, brand and insights manager, BP**

"Amantha is the master of making creativity genuinely democratic and highly contagious. In the same way that these creativity techniques and exercises are written for anyone to get their heads around and run with, they simply work bloody well, and have brought buckets of creative momentum and energy to OMD!"
— **Trudi Sampola, strategy director, OMD**

"Dr. Imber's advice on encouraging creativity is more than a bright and breezy discourse (which it certainly is). It is also readable, deceptively simple and highly practical. Drawing on tried and tested formulas, she covers fifty ways to push your creativity buttons, from getting intimate with strangers to the benefits of interruptions. I was particularly impressed with her chapter "Brainstorming is bollocks" which deals with — among other things — the fatuous concept that all ideas are good ideas. Imber is not a fan of feel good, consultant-style "fluffery". She wants the real thing — understandable, experience-based and do-able. These fifty exercises aimed at both individual and organisational level, are exactly that — fun, feasible and, if practised diligently, beneficial."
— **Tim Mendham, editor, *Fast Thinking***

The Creativity Formula:
50 scientifically-proven creativity boosters for work and for life

The Creativity Formula:
50 scientifically-proven creativity boosters for work and for life

Dr. Amantha Imber

Liminal Press

Published by Liminal Press
56 Almond St, Caulfield, VIC, Australia, 3162
www.liminalpress.com
info@liminalpress.com

First published by Liminal Press, 2009.

www.thecreativityformula.com
info@thecreativityformula.com

ISBN: 978-0-646-50962-4

Cover design by Acimovic Borivoje (aka OneCrazyDiamond)

Author photograph by Kris Growcott

Printed by Trojan Press

This book is dedicated to:

Those who don't feel they are creative but bought this book anyway. You are inspiring. Creativity involves moving into uncharted territories, taking a risk, finding what doesn't seem to be there. You have already taken the first step — enjoy the adventure.

Those who feel they are creative, but are open to learning new ways of being so. You have the insight to know that when the learning ends, the journey ends. I wish you a long, endlessly inventive and wondrous journey.

Table of Contents

Introduction

The problem with fluff

I have a pet hate — it's what I call 'fluff'. For me, fluff is the thousands of articles and books that put forward opinions, theories and models based on nothing more than one person's opinion, which have never been tested. Fluff is rife in the self-help, business and motivational sections of bookstores, where almost every book is filled with one-off case studies, senior managers' points of view on a topic or counsellors who got their degrees from cereal boxes.

Some of these books have been helpful to people, but the majority deliver 'knowledge' that unfortunately just does not work. It fails to work because often what we believe to be right intuitively is not, and can do more harm than good. Alternatively, it might be unhelpful because it isn't telling us anything we don't already know and therefore doesn't advance us.

Where you find fluff, you often also find allusions to 'creativity'. The topic of creativity tends to attract every man, woman and their dog, and quite often the goldfish will come along for the ride. Creativity is a field in which many self-proclaimed 'experts' lack formal qualifications or degrees. As a result, anyone can claim to be a creativity authority. You've worked as a senior innovation manager at a global internet company? Great, you can call yourself a creativity guru. You worked as an ad agency creative director making thirty-second TV commercials for the past decade? You can be Singapore's answer to Edward de Bono.

Certainly, there are some amazingly talented people in the field of creativity — and innovation. But there are also a lot of people who should have kept their day jobs.

Science-based creativity

It is because there is so much fluff posing as expertise in the field of creativity that I decided to write this book. I prefer science-based evidence. I believe in research where techniques have been tried and tested, re-worked and tested again, until they have been proven to significantly increase whatever it is they claim to increase. When I teach these techniques to participants in my workshops and training sessions, I can be 100% confident they actually work. And I love science because it is one of the few things you can rely on in this uncertain world.

In the case of creativity, thousands of scientific findings have been published in top-tier journal articles by researchers at some of the world's leading universities, such as Cornell, Harvard and NYU. Yet when I first started working in the creativity and innovation industry, I couldn't find a single person who was actually using these findings. So my mission became to give these findings life, to bring them into the public arena rather than keep them hidden in academia. I wanted to get these findings out there because they are valuable, teachable, practical, and they work. If you want to find out more, there's a reading list at the end of this book.

Where I'm coming from

Before I go any further, I should probably take a moment to introduce myself. Otherwise, I'm just someone with an unusual name.

As you might have suspected, I have a background in science; psychology, to be exact. I knew from an early age that I wanted to be a psychologist as I was fascinated by human behaviour. I studied psychology at Monash University in Melbourne, Australia and was the youngest person to graduate from its Doctorate of Organisational Psychology program, when I was twenty-five.

Creativity has always been a huge passion and focus for me. I illustrated my first book when I was eight (sure, my mother was the author, but they say in the publishing world it is all about who you know). I completed Spotlight's advanced sewing course when I was twelve and started making hats to sell in retail stores. When I was in my late teens, I became obsessed with playwriting and won a national award when I was nineteen. My playwriting turned into songwriting over the next couple of years and I was offered an international record deal for my first album when I was twenty-one. And then I moved into the world of advertising, to help create advertising strategies for many household brands.

While I have been researching creativity for more than ten years, I started officially working in the field about two years ago. I invented a company called Inventium. Through this company, my mission is to empower people to think more creatively. And specifically, to do this through science-based, tried and tested techniques.

I have helped all sorts of people, from those who truly believe they don't have a creative bone in their body to CEOs who specialise in innovation. I get my kicks from introducing people to tools that actually work and seeing how improving people's ability to think creatively increases their personal well-being and happiness as well as their enjoyment and productivity at work.

I have seen creativity training transform teams and cultures, and turn workplaces into energetic, fun places that people enjoy coming to. I have seen people who wear suits and think creativity is best left to the whacky folk in marketing come up with breakthrough ideas that transform their companies.

Common creativity myths

If you're reading this book, I probably don't need to sell you on the powers of creativity. But before I get into the rest of the book, I want to dispel some of the popular myths that surround creativity.

While working as a creativity consultant, I often hear people protesting that they are not creative. They think only geniuses like Shakespeare, Einstein and Picasso are truly creative. "What chance do we have of ever being that creative?" they ask. The answer is, they have an excellent chance, because everyone can think creatively.

To demonstrate, I will explain how ideas are formed. New ideas are formed when two existing thoughts in your brain combine in a new way. For example, when Bette Nesmith Graham was thinking about how to erase her typing mistakes more cleanly, she was also thinking about the fact that painters simply used paint to brush over their mistakes (no pun intended). These two thoughts connected and led to the idea of Liquid Paper. So if you have a brain which has thoughts floating around in it, you are fully capable of being creative.

Another myth is that creativity is a magical or random event. This myth developed through stories about Newton and the apple or Archimedes and the overflowing bath. Stories like these make people believe that creativity is out of their control or that they must sit around in baths and wait for inspiration to strike. Thankfully, the ability to be creative is something that can be taught. It has been shown to be that way in thousands of scientific experiments. This book is all about how you can be creative now, rather than at some random moment in the future.

Many organisations believe they will need to make big changes to create a culture that is conducive to creativity and innovation. Large-scale changes can help, but there are also many small things you can do that will have a big effect. This book contains many of those small changes that will actually make a significant difference to your organisation's creative output.

Hopefully I have convinced you that you have what it takes to be creative, even if you failed high school art class. And if you are already creative, you can become even more so.

Proven techniques only

What you are about to read is the product of thousands of studies on creativity — what increases it and what does not. This book only includes those findings which have been conclusively shown to increase creativity in conditions that are repeatable and demonstrably not due to chance. This book gives you the best of the best; the studies that produced the strongest results, which can be turned into practical ideas to turbo-charge creativity in your work and personal life.

It is important to add that these studies are not just about abstract laboratory statistics; they involve techniques that work in real life. All of the fifty methods in this book have been used at various times by my clients and students and have achieved very positive results.

This book also makes practical suggestions you can apply immediately to increase your creativity. These real-world suggestions are based on scientific findings, where the information is both functional and effective. There's a reference list at the end of the book which details the research relevant to each chapter. You can be sure it works because scientists have already done the testing.

Individual and organisation-wide creativity

This book can be used by individuals or whole organisations. Many organisations realise they must innovate to survive, but don't know where to start. This book will help create a culture of innovation in which creative thinking and solutions become the norm. This is a fundamental step to becoming a truly innovative organisation.

This book is also aimed at individuals who want to think more creatively. You might want to do this in the context of your work or personal life. It is also for people who don't feel creative but would love to be more so. This book will help you get in touch with your own creativity and learn some simple ways to become more creative.

Each chapter has specific tips for individuals and organisations — just read the ones that apply to your needs.

You can read this book in two different ways. If you're a traditionalist, you can go from cover to cover. The fifty findings that boost creativity in the book have been organised in a way that makes chronological sense. Alternatively, you can dip into random bits while you have a spare ten minutes on the train. This book works equally well by picking random chapters to read and digest at your leisure.

Fitting creativity into the everyday

The findings in this book can be used individually or in combination. Any of these ideas will significantly improve your creativity. That said, the more of them you apply, the more creative you and your organisation will become.

It is important to note that this book is designed to complement what you are already doing. I believe in the saying "if it ain't broke, don't fix it". If your organisation has already put in place initiatives which have significantly increased creativity and innovation, please do not change them. But if you are currently not doing anything to boost creativity or would like do to more, this book gives you a great starting point.

I encourage you to take what you like from this book, particularly those ideas you think you could realistically and quickly implement. As for the rest, leave it behind if it does not appeal. Alternatively, you could challenge yourself to incorporate one finding per week for a whole year, which would certainly turbo-charge creativity within your organisation. Or you could pick a finding at random every few days and commit to implementing it at work or in life.

However you decide to use this book, I can assure you that all fifty of these findings will significantly boost your creativity. So please, enjoy the journey and enjoy the forthcoming ideas.

Meet Fred, Emma, Jason and Amy

I would like you to meet Fred, Emma, Jason and Amy. While you don't know any of these people personally, you probably know someone like them.

Fred works at a large chocolate manufacturing company. He works in the marketing department and was recently promoted to senior brand manager for chocolate bars. He looks after the marketing for several of the bars you see at your local supermarkets and convenience stores. Some people would call this a dream job. Fred thinks it's pretty cool, although he has put on a few pounds in the last twelve months from too much 'product sampling'.

Amy works in the human resources department at a big financial services company. She looks after staff learning and development and has been there for a couple of years now. The culture is a pretty conservative one — no surprises there, it's a bank. But the organisation is very supportive of staff development, which makes Amy's life much easier. Typically, Amy designs and runs programs for basic skills such as leadership, presentation and negotiation. However, lately she has been reading about the importance of having staff members who are effective creative problem solvers. The bank lists 'innovation' as one of its values, although Amy is yet to witness how it puts this into practice.

Jason runs a small retail business. He and his three staff members sell a range of electronic goods in the city. He is focused on selling as many products as possible to all those who enter his store. He thinks innovation is probably more important to his suppliers, who make all the cool gadgets he sells, and is not 100% sure how it applies to him and his goal of selling more product.

Emma works as an account manager in an advertising agency. Her days are spent coming up with strategies and advertising campaigns that will help her clients sell more products. Emma likes the fast-paced, high-stress work environment but she still sees many of her co-workers having 'creative blocks' and struggling to come up with yet another brilliant campaign idea.

You'll get to learn more about these four people as you read on though the book, and hear about their struggles and successes to think creatively and drive innovation within their respective organisations.

So please, enjoy the journey and look forward to being able to turbo-charge your creative thinking abilities when you come out the other end.

1

Have you warmed up your brain?

CHAPTER 1

IT'S 6 A.M. AND JASON IS WALKING bleary-eyed to the gym. He has just started a new exercise regime and is trying doggedly to stick to it despite not being a morning person.

He arrives at the gym, walks up the stairs and hops onto the treadmill for his standard five-minute warm-up. His legs start moving underneath him, his body temperature rises and slowly he starts to become fully conscious. After five minutes, Jason is warmed up and ready for a workout.

For those of us who exercise regularly, doing a big workout without a warm-up seems silly. Our risk of injury increases and it also makes it hard for us to perform at our best.

Similarly, it is critical to warm up your brain before engaging it in a creative-thinking workout. This is to combat the fact that in general, most idea-generation and problem-solving meetings are scheduled immediately after a strategy or finance meeting, in which your brain was most likely in analytical or linear gear.

Most of us can appreciate how difficult it is to come from a meeting that requires analytical, rational thinking into a meeting that requires us to think laterally (that is, thinking outside of our usual frame of reference).

When your brain has been in linear thinking mode, coming up with creative solutions is very difficult. The brain naturally wants to jump to logical solutions, given the mode it is in, and finding lateral and creative solutions becomes unnecessarily difficult.

Scientific research suggests that warming up the creative-thinking parts of your brain will help you perform more effectively and efficiently at creative tasks. These exercises will make it easier to jump from a finance meeting to an idea-generation meeting.

Warming up this part of your brain only takes a few minutes to shift your brain into an open-minded and lateral-thinking mode.

There are many ways to warm up your brain to this type of thinking. One is an Inventium tool called Fat Chance.

Fat Chance was designed with the specific purpose of warming up the creative-thinking parts of people's brains. The tool can be used before thirty-minute idea-generation and problem-solving workshops or one-day blue-sky think-ing workshops in which brains need to think laterally for an entire day.

Fat Chance requires no materials or stimuli other than one thing: an impossible challenge. For example, cure cancer by lunchtime tomorrow.

There are two key elements to creating an impossible challenge. The first is to pick a goal or an objective that is almost impossible to achieve with technology as we know it today. The second is to add an incredibly tight time frame. The tighter the better. For example, Raise Paris Hilton's IQ by 100 points by the end of the week. Give birth to an alien by dinner tonight. Marry Brad Pitt by noon tomorrow.

After you have developed an impossible challenge, the next step is to divide the participants into pairs or groups of three. This gives everyone a good chance to participate.

Once groups are assigned, instruct people to generate at least three solutions to the problem in five minutes. Encourage those who are finding it difficult and remind them that the solutions do not have to be logical or rational — in fact, those solutions won't actually solve the problem.

After these five minutes have passed, you can feel confident that the divergent thinking parts of people's brains will be sufficiently warmed up.

Why does this tool work so effectively? It all comes back to the impossibility of the challenge. Given that it is impossible, non-creative thinking will not lead to a solution. The problem can only be solved through taking a leap and thinking very creatively and laterally.

For example, in relation to the Paris Hilton problem, some solutions might include bribing the instructor for the answers, making the IQ test about fashion rather than general knowledge, or finding another person named Paris Hilton who happens to be very smart. Despite the 'craziness' of these problems and answers, groups have then gone on to generate innovative solutions to real life problems they were facing.

For individuals:

- When you are aware that a task requires creative or lateral thought, take five minutes to warm up your brain by first creating an impossible challenge, and then challenging yourself to generate at least three solutions.

 For organisations:

- Before starting a meeting or workshop that requires creative thought, take the group through the Fat Chance warm-up activity. Provide an impossible challenge and divide the room into groups of two or three and ask them to generate at least three solutions in five minutes.

2

Don't worry, be happy

W E DON'T OFTEN THINK ABOUT the effect our emotions have on our ability to think or do work. At Fred's organisation, management believes that emotional states have very little to do with productivity.

Our emotional state, in fact, has a big impact on our ability to think creatively. Researchers at Pennsylvania State University conducted a study which examined the impact of happy and sad moods on idea generation. To put them into the required mood, participants were first asked to describe a recent life event that made them feel happy or sad. Following the mood manipulation, participants were asked to write down as many things as they could think of that could fly. On average, participants in the happy group came up with almost 50% more ideas than the sad group.

The happiness hypothesis was also explored by Teresa Amabile at Harvard University. Amabile asked several hundred people to keep a work diary that detailed their daily activities, moods and other workplace events. An analysis of these diary entries showed that people were more likely to come up with breakthrough ideas when they were feeling happy, even if this happiness was experienced the day before the idea was generated.

When we are happy, the level of a brain chemical called dopamine increases. In the frontal lobe, dopamine controls the flow of information to other parts of the brain. When people feel happy, thoughts or images of one concept — such as 'thick' — activate thoughts or images of many other concepts — such as 'paint', 'stupid' or 'make-up'. Opening up connections between concepts that are only remotely associated with one another increases our ability for divergent thinking. In contrast, when people feel sad, they become more detail-oriented with their thinking which means that they often will not see the greater possibilities. In other words, they get focused on the trees to the exclusion of the forest.

So if you are feeling a bit flat, chances are you are probably not performing at your peak creativity. The common image of the 'tortured genius' has fed the popular belief that the majority of creative geniuses were depressed and emotionally unbalanced. However, studies have shown that people are actually more creative when they're happy.

🚶 For individuals:

- Before embarking on a task that requires you to be creative, try to imagine a time when you were really happy.
- Monitor your emotions closely and time creative tasks with your emotional state. Whenever you find yourself feeling happy, take out the creative project you're working on. Likewise, if you're feeling a bit down, leave the creative task for another time.

For organisations:

- Provide employees with a workplace they are happy to come to. For example, working conditions and policies should be flexible enough to incorporate all types of people, and part of the focus for work should be on having fun.
- In workshops or meetings where creative thought needs to occur, warm people up by screening an episode of a mainstream comedy that will be sure to put people in a positive mood.

3

Straitjackets can be good

A MY ALWAYS THOUGHT CONSTRAINTS and param-
eters were bad when it came to idea generation. Free
expression makes creative juices flow, or at least that's
the message her high school art teacher left her with.

Letting your mind wander wherever it needs to,
starting with a blank canvas and being free of rules
are all considered conducive to creativity. However,
the latest psychological research has shown the complete opposite.

In one study, a group of adults was asked to make
a construction using LEGO™ One group was given
no constraints; they were told that they could build
whatever they liked. The other group had several
constraints placed upon them; they were told that
their construction must contain no right-angled joints
and they could only use one kind of brick.

The constructions built by the 'constraints' group
were judged to be significantly more creative and lateral
than those in the 'free expression' group.

So why does this happen? When completing tasks, we typically draw on what we know rather than seeking new ideas and opinions. Often, information retrieval becomes automated in our brains because it is useful and saves us having to come up with new solutions every time we face a problem. In other words, when we are assigned a task to complete, our brains switch into autopilot if it is a familiar problem.

However, this autopilot mode dramatically impairs performance when we have to think of completely novel ideas. Constraining the way we think forces us to search for new and creative ways of completing the task or solving the problem. In a paradoxical way, putting constraints on our tasks lifts the constraints on our thought processing.

For individuals:

- Try to avoid taking on tasks that are open-ended and overly broad. If you find yourself in this situation, challenge yourself to apply a constraint to the task to make yourself perform more creatively.
- Whenever you feel yourself going into autopilot, ask your boss to apply a constraint to the task (or do it yourself).

For organisations:

- Try challenging your team to a task that has a constraint this week. Ask them to create a presentation without PowerPoint or express an idea without speaking.
- Whenever you assign people specific projects that require creativity, make sure you give them at least one or two constraints.

4

Bring on the newbies

CHAPTER 4

M OST OF US HAVE BEEN a victim of groupthink
at some stage in our working lives. If you have
been sitting with the same team for the past year,
you've probably also become a victim of 'team-think'.
Emma has worked with some teams on advertising
projects where it felt as if discussions of new problems,
such as driving awareness for a product, would inevitably come back to the same old core set of answers.

This happens a lot in companies that deal with
similar problems for their various clients. I work with
several advertising and media agencies and often
the key issue for many of their clients is generating
awareness for their products. When the agency tries
to generate ideas on how to do this, the strategies tend
to revolve around the same few media channels, such
as TV, print and outdoor campaigns, or creating a
viral video and posting it on YouTube.

Research suggests that teams which have been
together for a while develop a set of entrenched

assumptions, ways of doing things and set patterns of behaviour. The good news is there is a cure: introducing a new member to the team. Studies show that when a new member joins a team, existing assumptions, attitudes and behaviours are far less likely to be activated. The new person triggers new thoughts and behaviours.

While it can be tempting to leave harmonious teams alone, rotating employees around to different teams regularly, say every six to eight months, can considerably enhance creativity.

When I run idea-generation sessions for clients, I almost always insist they invite people who do not work for their company. I encourage them to include as diverse a mix of people as possible. For example, in one workshop for a national postal services organisation, we had the artistic director of a circus troupe, a creative director from an advertising agency, an eighteen-year-old university student and a TV host. Needless to say, the ideas generated in the workshop were wonderfully varied.

🏃 For individuals:

- Rather than try to think creatively on your own, try to partner up with someone you don't normally work with. Use them as a springboard for fleshing out your ideas and let them go in directions you wouldn't if you were working on your own. Most importantly, listen to their input and be open to going in directions you would not normally.

🏃🏃 For organisations:

- Try to invite people from outside your team or department to all idea-generation meetings and workshops.
- For the larger idea-generation workshops, invite people who are external to the organisation and have no obvious connection to the problems that need to be solved.

5
Broad horizons

TAKE A MINUTE TO THINK about the people you know whom you consider to be really creative. Chances are, they have had quite broad experiences in their lives and exposed themselves to a wide range of stimuli.

One of Jason's closest friends, Tom, works as an illustrator at a graphics design firm. Tom's weeks are normally full of extracurricular activities, such as wandering through the latest art exhibition at his local gallery, going to see a visiting professor speak at the university or immersing himself in a book on a topic he knows nothing about. And when Jason thinks about it, it is normally Tom who sends him the most bizarre and funny clips and articles over email, as opposed to any of his 'less creative' friends.

Scientists have studied whether exposure to a wide range of information increases divergent thinking abilities. In a study conducted at Drake University, Maria Clapham tested the hypothesis that diverse stimuli would increase creative thought. They asked one group of people to undertake an idea-generation task without being exposed to any stimulus prior to the task. A second group of people were required to read a list of sixty random, unrelated pieces of information and then complete the idea-generation task. Those in the latter group performed significantly better.

These findings suggest that exposure to lots of unrelated information gets the creative juices flowing. Indeed, the more thoughts and experiences you have floating around in your brain, the greater the chance of having creative and lateral thoughts.

Apple founder Steve Jobs told a group of Stanford University graduates how exposure to seemingly irrelevant stimuli was a trigger for one of the company's key points of difference. Jobs dropped out of university because he was sick of taking classes that didn't interest him. Afterward he decided to attend classes that actually looked interesting. One course that caught his eye was calligraphy and Reed College, where he studied, had one of the country's best calligraphy courses. So he enrolled.

During the course Jobs learned all about typefaces, the difference between serif and sans-serif fonts and how to create beautiful lettering. At the time, he had no idea how this course would have any application in his life. However, years later when he was designing the very first Macintosh computer, it all came back to him. Macs became the first computers to be full of beautiful typefaces — one of the hallmarks of the Apple brand.

The gift card company Hallmark has taken to heart the principle of wide exposure to information. Every year, it invites over fifty speakers to its Kansas City headquarters. Past guests have included Cirque De Soleil founder Guy Laliberté, ex-Apple Fellow and venture capitalist Guy Kawasaki and poet David Whyte. The purpose of bringing these speakers in is to stimulate the 740 artists, designers, writers, editors and photographers who generate over 15,000 original greeting card designs every year.

🚶 For individuals:

- At least once a week, challenge yourself to do something you wouldn't normally do.
- See a genre of film that you wouldn't normally gravitate to.
- Attend a public lecture on a topic you know nothing about.
- Try cooking a meal you have never cooked before.
- Randomly select a short course to attend.

For organisations:

- Assign different members of your team to email around one random fact per day.
- Try pinning up a different article every day on the back of the restroom door (giving people an opportunity to read it when they have the time and inclination).
- Ensure employees subscribe to at least one trend-spotting newsletter, such as trendcentral.com, to ensure they are aware of different things going on in the outside world.
- Introduce show-and-tell sessions to regular meetings. Ask everyone in the team to speak for a few minutes about a topic they are passionate about or a trend or other piece of information they have learned about during the week.
- Think beyond job-related competencies in your company's learning and development strategy and train staff members in skills that don't relate to their job in any obvious way.
- Team excursions are an efficient and inexpensive way of exposing people to diverse information. For example, you could spend the last Friday afternoon of every month taking your team to the latest exhibition or attending a public lecture.

6

Warm me up

Amy works in a high rise building in the CBD. She takes the train to work and only has to walk a couple of blocks from the station before she is at the foyer of the thirty-two-storey building. As she takes the lift up to the fourteenth floor, she never really gives too much thought to the walls, doors and windows that surround her. And why should she? It's not as if the physical environment of a workplace has an impact on the bottom line or anything.

Recent research suggests the opposite: your physical surroundings have a huge impact on your creative thinking skills and innovation. This in turn impacts an organisation's bottom line in a very big way.

Warm colours, for example red and orange, promote divergent thinking. In a study conducted at Cornell University, people were exposed to both warm- and cool-coloured environments. The researchers asked people to complete a creativity task while in these environments. Those people in the warm-coloured environment performed significantly better on this creativity task, suggesting that warm-coloured environments help foster creativity.

This effect occurs because warm colours tend to make us feel happier than cooler colours. And when we are happy, a chemical called dopamine is released in our brains, which makes information flow more freely. Encouraging free-flowing thoughts in your brain is a neurological way to increase idea generation and lateral thinking skills.

 ### For individuals:

- Paint the surface of your desk a warm colour such as orange, yellow or red.
- Pin a warm-coloured poster above your desk.
- Purchase a couple of small warm-coloured items, such as a pen holder and mug, for your desk.
- Buy a yellow desk lamp.
- For your next idea-generation session, make sure everyone writes down their ideas on red, orange and yellow pieces of paper.
- Replace all plain manila folders with warm colours.

 ### For organisations:

- Paint some warm-coloured feature walls.
- Change some of the office fixtures and accessories to warm colours.
- Only purchase warm-coloured furniture.

Natural goodness

A s Fred sits at his desk trying to work, his gaze is intermittently caught by the view from his window. His building faces a large park in the city. Whenever Fred is stuck for a thought, he lets his gaze, and his mind, wander to this outside world.

If you sit close to a window and like letting your eyes rest on the natural scenery outside, you are doing wonders for your creativity.

Several scientific studies have compared the effects of an office with or without nature, or even a view of it. Creativity was significantly higher in the 'natural' offices. People thought the environment was more conducive to creativity and also performed better in an idea-generation task.

There are a number of reasons why natural environments improve creative thought. First, there is research to suggest that natural environments relieve stress. Stress and anxiety are both big barriers for creative thought. Reducing this barrier can help release

---

19

creative energy. There is much evidence that people who are more relaxed are better at processing abstract information, hence at thinking creatively.

The natural environment is also less structured than our offices. In general, unstructured environments enhance creativity because they contain more stimuli for creative thought. In addition, natural environments are less constraining, promoting the feeling of freedom.

 ### For individuals:

- Ask for a desk with a nice view.
- If that doesn't work, go out during your lunch break to buy a pot plant and place it on your desk.
- Invest in a Japanese water fountain to place on the side of your desk.

 ### For organisations:

- When choosing an office to rent, prioritise those with views of the outside world.
- Avoid furniture made from plastic or synthetic materials. Instead, try to pick furniture that is made from natural materials, such as wood.
- Pin up some pictures of rainforests and waterfalls on the wall.

8

When less is less

THANKS TO ARCHITECTS SUCH AS Ludwig Mies van der Rohe, the term 'less is more' became an aspiration for designers from the 1960s until today. We have all seen, and perhaps lived or worked in, environments with plenty of space but very little furniture or trimmings.

Emma used to like the modern, minimalist office she works in, but now she finds it a bit lifeless. Even if minimalism is your cup of tea, stark environments are very bad for creativity.

One of the best ways to provoke creative thought is to surround the brain with lots of diverse stimuli. This increases the number of connections sparked in the brain, and therefore the number of new ideas popping up. An office that has the bare minimum of furniture and accessories will not provide much stimulus to drive creative thought.

It is ironic that many 'creative' companies, such as advertising agencies and design firms, pay high prices for minimalist, sleek looking offices to make clients think they are cutting-edge, creative and contemporary. In fact, such environments make it much harder for employees to think creatively.

An environment that contains many objects and textures is much more conducive than a stark, minimalist one to lateral thinking. Offices that have exposed pipes, asymmetric lines and unusual and varied furniture are very effective at driving lateral thinking. Likewise, offices that have lots of artwork or posters covering the walls or odd and interesting bits and pieces such as an Elvis figurine suctioned to the window, are excellent drivers of creative thought. (And yes, I was in an office yesterday that had a suction-cup Elvis hanging from the window.)

 ### For individuals:

- Take a trip to your local bargain furniture retailer to pick up some inexpensive, bright and unusual bits and pieces to fill your office space.
- Your local opportunity shop can also be great for hunting down some quirky and interesting treasures.
- Create an office toy box.

 ### For organisations:

- Find a designer who will add some interesting quirks to your office space and make it interesting, rather than sleek.
- If your current office has a minimalist design, order more furniture and other pieces of stimulating decorations.

Water-cooler creativity

A MY SITS IN YOUR TYPICAL 2×2-metre cubicle space in her white-walled office. All forms of social life tend to be blocked out by her cubicle walls. This is ideal on the days she needs to concentrate on a task that requires attention to detail. However, this work environment is also hindering her creativity.

Creativity scientists Janetta McCoy and Gary Evans researched the effect of social workplaces. They asked people to rate the creative potential of a number of different working environments. One variable they examined in this study was the extent to which the environments helped facilitate social interaction. The study revealed that people rated social environments to be much more creativity-friendly.

In another study, McCoy and Evans had participants complete a task that required creative thinking. Half of the participants were in a highly social environment, while the other group sat in a space which was not conducive to sociability. Participants exposed to the social environment performed 33% more creatively on the task, as assessed by a team of independent judges. The researchers concluded that at least one important design variable for a workspace is how much it can increase social interaction.

So according to research, workspaces that provide opportunities for social interaction are generally rated more creativity-friendly by staff members and also tend to be more beneficial for innovation.

Comfortable furniture arranged in a circle invites gatherings and social interaction. This interaction can increase opportunities to share ideas and insights.

Informal meeting areas also make an environment more conducive to social interaction. When you have many informal meeting areas, this unconsciously signals to employees that discussion is encouraged. I have found that when organisations have informal meeting places, these spaces get used effectively. Even talking about last night's episode of the latest reality TV show can be an effective use of time if it gets lots of different thoughts firing in the brain, which could later trigger a solution to a current problem.

 ### For individuals:

- Create an informal meeting area near your desk by scattering a few beanbags.

 ### For organisations:

- Ensure your workplace has areas for talking and sharing.
- Place desks facing each other to allow for easy social interaction.
- Include lots of informal meeting areas in your floor space design.
- Make sure partitions are low enough to allow people to talk to the person opposite them.

10
Breaking the rules

JASON IS A HUGE FAN OF the TV series *The Young Ones*. He constantly finds ways to fit quotes from the show into everyday conversation with his workmates. Resident punk Vyvyan was his favourite character so it makes sense that Jason has a poster of Vyvyan above his desk at the back of his store.

When Jason initially put the poster up, he had no idea that it could impact on his creativity. It may seem strange to think that staring at a poster of an eccentric fictional character can make you significantly more creative, but that is exactly what a group of researchers across several universities in America and Germany discovered.

Jens Forster and his colleagues were interested in the concept of 'breaking the rules' and 'being different from the norm' and its effect on creativity. More specifically, they hypothesised that objects or pictures relating to the concept of 'being different' in some way were likely to promote divergent thinking (that is, the ability to think creatively).

They tested this hypothesis in a study in which participants were allocated to one of two groups. Participants in Group 1 were seated in front of a poster that had sixteen letter Xs of the same colour arranged in a 4×4 matrix. Those in Group 2 were seated in front of a similar poster where one of the Xs was a different colour than the rest. All participants were then asked to come up with as many uses for a brick as they could think of.

Those who were seated in front of the 'odd one out' poster came up with significantly more ideas than the 'conformity' group. In addition, the 'odd one out' group's ideas were independently judged as being around 25% more creative than the 'conformity' group.

The researchers explained that the differently coloured X in the poster activated unconscious thoughts about breaking the rules and originality. And activating these thoughts fosters a greater quality and quantity of ideas.

🚶 *For individuals:*

- Find some posters that relate to 'standing out', 'originality' or 'eccentricity' and put them up around your desk and on the walls of your workplace.

🚶🚶 *For organisations:*

- Put up pictures of concepts relating to being 'different' in meeting and workshop rooms that are used for sessions that require creative thought.
- Likewise, put these types of pictures in corridors and office walls to consistently activate thoughts of originality in employees.

11

Up for a challenge

TAKE A MINUTE TO REFLECT on the week you've just completed at work. Think about each day and the types of tasks you were doing and consider how challenging or easy each project was to complete.

When Jason first started his retail business, he found it very challenging as he had never run his own company before. Everything was new; everything required a steep learning curve and few things came automatically or particularly easily. During these first few months, he contributed some of his best thinking and ideas to the company he was building. This was no coincidence.

One of the strongest predictors of creativity in the workplace is whether employees feel adequately challenged by their jobs. Those who feel their jobs are challenging and that the objectives and goals they are set stretch their capabilities are more likely to behave more creatively.

This effect is enhanced when employees are allowed to work autonomously, rather than being given step-by-step, day-by-day instructions on how to reach these goals. Creative behaviour occurs when employees have the freedom to work out for themselves how to reach their challenging targets.

However, it is important that employees do not feel too stretched, as this can lead to frustration. Likewise, not feeling stretched enough can lead to boredom.

If you are a manager, take a moment to reflect on how you instruct the people who work for you to go about doing tasks. Consider how detailed your instructions are, and whether you allow room for movement.

At Fred's organisation, matching projects to employees is not something that tends to take priority. Instead, it is simply a matter of working out who is up to their eyeballs in work and who has time to take on extra work. However, this traditional approach to task allocation hinders creativity.

The assignment of tasks needs to be based instead on skill level, and whether the employee would feel challenged by the task. A task should be assigned to an employee who can understand the task and not be completely daunted by it. Likewise the task should challenge them and not be too simple for them to complete. Assigning the right task to the right person ensures that they feel stimulated by their work.

In addition, consider assigning tasks based on interest. This requires understanding the types of projects employees like and matching available tasks to the employees' interests.

If you match tasks in this way, you will find employees deliver much better results. Creative thought will increase and employee satisfaction will skyrocket, because people will be more intrinsically motivated to complete tasks.

For individuals:

- If you don't feel as if you are currently being challenged enough by your work, ask your manager to provide more challenging tasks.
- If you are receiving very detailed instructions on how to complete assigned tasks, ask your manager to tone down the detail of the instructions and leave the 'how' part up to you.

 For organisations:

- Consider assigning tasks based on employees' interests as well as their current workload, experience or capabilities.
- Always ask for feedback from your staff to check that they are feeling adequately challenged by their jobs.

12

Joining the dots

I WANT YOU TO THINK ABOUT the word 'dog'. Next, spend twenty seconds writing down any words that come to mind when you think of 'dog'.

In general, there are two types of responses to this task. Some people consistently produce a few closely related words, such as cat, bark and fur. Other people are able to produce a large number of words, some of which are only remotely associated with the target word, such as He-Man, carpet, fence and Mars.

People who consistently produce a few closely related words have what neurologists call 'steep associative hierarchies'. Their brains activate fewer, more closely associated, concepts at the same time. People who have steep associative hierarchies have a reduced chance of naturally developing creative associations.

In contrast, people who generate a large number of words, some of which are only remotely associated with the target word, have what is called 'flat associative hierarchies'. In their brains, these people have weaker connections between close concepts and stronger connections between more remote concepts. Because these brains activate a large number of distantly related concepts at the same time, they have a much greater chance of developing unusual and creative associations.

The good news is that we can all join the flat-associative-hierarchies group with minimal effort and a tiny bit of stimulus.

Activating remotely associated concepts in your brain is simple: all you need to do is expose yourself to concepts that are different and unrelated to the target concept. By exposing yourself to diverse concepts, you increase the likelihood of making creative associations.

Maria Clapham at Drake University researched the effect of exposure to unrelated concepts on creativity. She split participants into two groups. Group 1 was exposed to several random sentences, such as 'Utah is the beehive state' and 'At low tide, the hulk of the old ship could be seen.' Group 2 received no stimulus. Following this, both groups had to participate in an idea-generation task. Clapham found that those in Group 1 performed significantly better in the creativity task than did Group 2. Clapham concluded that this result was due to the random stimuli activating different concepts in participants' brains, which gave way to more novel connections and ideas.

Fred's company wants to generate an idea for a new chocolate bar that will appeal to the female market. To help his team generate a creative idea, Fred introduced a completely unrelated concept into the equation that had to be incorporated into the idea in some way. Fred's random idea was a vacuum cleaner. By linking these two concepts, chocolate bar and vacuum cleaner, Fred and his co-workers generated novel ideas for a new product. For example, the new product could be a fat-busting 'diet' chocolate bar that has the ability to actively break down and suck away fat. I know that I would buy it!

 For individuals:

- Before undertaking a task that requires creative thinking, expose yourself to several unrelated concepts. Take a walk outside and consciously look at objects that have nothing to do with the task at hand. Once you are back inside, force yourself to find a solution to the task by linking one of the unrelated objects to the task at hand.

For organisations:

- Fill your workplace, particularly meeting rooms where creative thinking needs to occur, with random bits of stimuli. Toys can be very effective for this, as they tend to activate many different concepts in the brain. For example, you might put together a toy box for every meeting room that employees can dip into whenever they have to embark on a creative thinking task.

13

I don't want your money, honey

THINK BACK OVER THE PAST few years and consider how your performance at work has been rewarded. If you're like most people, you probably received cash bonuses based on your performance against sales, profit or market share. The majority of companies have complex systems of remuneration based on your contribution to the bottom line.

Jason rewards his staff with cash bonuses when they sell a certain number of products, in addition to performance on several other metrics. This reward system may make it easier for Jason's staff to meet their monthly mortgage repayments, but it hinders their creativity.

Many universities and researchers around the world have studied pay-for-performance reward systems. In one such study, researchers from Harvard University examined the effect of rewarding people with money for performance, such as meeting sales targets. They found that individuals who were rewarded in this manner tended to avoid risky behaviour. People got so caught up in achieving their targets, they focused on repeating what they had done in the past and tried not to do anything that might mess up their rewards.

When people try to avoid risk, creativity is one of the first things to fly out the window. Creativity and innovation, of course, require a degree of risk and often a large number of failures before the breakthrough leap forward.

For individuals:

- If you are currently being rewarded with pay for performance, ask your boss whether this system can be changed. Let your boss understand that your reward system is having a negative effect on creativity and suggest that you should be rewarded for displaying competencies that are related to creativity and innovation, such as experimentation, open-mindedness and conscientiousness.

For organisations:

- Avoid rewarding employees with cash for performance on tasks that require creative thinking such as the development and launch of a new product or service.

14

A pat on the back

Rewarding employees with money helps them move up the corporate ladder and struggle less with monthly bills and mortgage repayments. However, as we saw in the last chapter, it is not the most effective way to motivate staff members. This is good news for people like Emma, who knows that her advertising agency would never dream of awarding cash bonuses to anyone.

Frederic Hertzberg, an extremely successful workplace psychologist, spent years examining the different types of motivation at work. He found that motivation fell into two categories: extrinsic and intrinsic.

Extrinsic motivation is driven by external factors, such as salary, job security and fringe benefits such as a company car. He termed these factors 'hygiene factors' because they do not effectively motivate people or increase job satisfaction when present, but when absent, they decrease job satisfaction significantly.

Intrinsic motivation is driven by internal factors and feelings, such as being challenged in a job, having responsibility and being recognised for one's work and achievements. Hertzberg found intrinsic motivation was highly related to job satisfaction. Researchers later found that intrinsic motivation was significantly related to one's ability to think creatively at work.

Recognising employees for their achievements and contributions will go a lot further than monetary rewards in keeping staff satisfied and increasing their ability and motivation to think creatively at work.

You can recognise staff members in a number of different ways. Some of my clients have annual awards ceremonies in which people who have contributed great ideas to the company are crowned Innovator of the Year. Others award an idea of the month and the winner receives a voucher for his or her efforts and is publicised through the internal company newsletter or intranet.

Another way to recognise employees' creative performance is by giving them more responsibility. Responsibility makes people happier at work and increases creativity.

For individuals:

- If your organisation currently does not recognise ideas and creative thinking, suggest to your manager that he or she should implement a recognition system.

For organisations:

- If your organisation places more emphasis on monetary rewards, consider tipping the balance to recognition. A recognition program will be much more powerful than money in motivating employees and encouraging them to think creatively.

15

Your CV looks great, but can you think?

CHAPTER 15

I WANT YOU TO TAKE A MINUTE to reflect on how you were recruited for your current job. If you're like most people, you were probably shortlisted by a recruiter or headhunter and invited in for a chat with your prospective boss. If you're in a senior position, you probably also had chats with the entire management team.

If you're like Amy and work for a large organisation, you may also have been through a battery of tests, including numerical and verbal reasoning and personality assessments. Amy felt all tested out by the time the organisation decided to offer her a job.

In advertising, an industry that lives or dies by how creative its people are, recruiting is almost solely conducted through chats with potential employees. If you are on the recruiting side, you probably get a good feel for people during these chats, although first impressions can be misleading. You might get to hear about the award-winning campaigns the applicant worked on and now claims to have been instrumental in creating. And you might even get to hear about their extra-curricular hobbies.

But take a step back and ask yourself, what are the most important qualities for staff members who will help set your company apart from the rest? The ability to think originally and creatively must be near the top, if not in prime position.

Why then do the majority of companies not test for creativity in the recruitment process? Sure, we might ask for past experiences at work-related tasks and key achievements. But this doesn't really tell us anything, given it is almost impossible to know how much input the candidate actually had.

Instead of endless chatting, companies need to change their recruitment processes to bring in more creative staff. Organisations need to gear the process around testing applicants' ability to think.

Testing people's ability to think originally will start to dramatically increase your organisation's overall creativity. In addition, by injecting highly creative people into the mix, existing employees will start to mirror the behaviour of these new people. Their creativity should be contagious.

Next time you set out to recruit a new staff member, place priority on working out whether he or she can think.

🏃 For individuals:

- Suggest to your manager that he or she change your company's recruitment strategy to test how candidates think. This will ensure you can work with stimulating people who will help your own creative thoughts.

 *For organisations:*

- You can test people's ability to think in a number of different ways. The simplest approach is to leave candidates alone in a room for half an hour with a problem your company is currently struggling with. Take away their lifelines (such as mobile phones) and leave them with a pen and a piece of paper. Come back into the room after thirty minutes have passed and ask them to explain their solution. Most importantly, ask them to describe how they arrived at the solution. This will provide the most insight into their thinking style and ability.

- For a more involved test, ask the candidate to solve a problem with a couple of his or her prospective team members. This will give you a feel for how candidates think and also how well they collaborate to solve problems.

- For a more formal approach, some of the world's most innovative companies use puzzles when they recruit. To find some examples, read *How Would You Move Mount Fuji?* by William Poundstone, which exposes how Microsoft and many Silicon Valley start-ups recruit the best, brightest and most creative thinkers.

16

Don't box me in

A T FRED'S WORKPLACE, people often get labelled. For example, one member of his team is the 'hard working one', another is 'the brains of the group', while another member is the 'class clown' who can always be relied on for lunchtime entertainment. This labelling might be done in jest (albeit with a grain or two of truth thrown in), but it can damage individual performance and self belief.

Emma remembers her first day working for an advertising agency, when she was introduced to all the different departments: production, account service, strategy and research and the creative department. Hang on...the creative department?

For me, one of the most bizarre aspects of advertising agencies is that they have a department labelled 'creative'. Creative departments are usually staffed by art directors and copywriters who are responsible for coming up with the ideas you see in advertisements. This department justifies the existence of most advertising agencies, but generally only accounts for 20–30% of an agency's employees. Does this mean the other 80% are support staff? Wouldn't an organisation work more effectively and efficiently if the rest of the people were also encouraged to think creatively?

Psychologists have found that when you give people a label, they tend to live up to it. For example, psychologist Gustav Jahoda examined the lives of the Ashanti people in central Ghana. In this culture, children are given a spiritual name that is based on the day they are born. Those born on a Monday are given the name Kwadwo, which is associated with being quiet and peaceful, while those born on a Wednesday are given the name Kwaku, which is associated with bad behaviour. To examine whether spiritual names had an impact on actual behaviour, Jahoda studied the number of times people born on different days appeared in the juvenile court records. He found that those born on a Wednesday appeared significantly more often than those born on a Monday. This study is one of many that demonstrates that a label can affect behaviour in very deep and enduring ways. The same holds true in the workplace: if you are labelled creative, chances are you will consider yourself creative and start to act that way.

🚶 **For individuals:**

- If you want to think creatively, start to label yourself as a creative thinker. This simple reframe will significantly increase your performance on tasks requiring creativity.

For organisations:

- Organisations need to resist labelling one department above all others 'creative'. By doing so, the rest of your staff will feel significantly more motivated and confident in suggesting an idea of their own.
- On the flipside, if you want your employees to think creatively, start to label everyone a creative person.

17

Why everyone can be a 'creative type'

IN THE PREVIOUS CHAPTER, we talked about the power of labelling. You can actually take this concept much deeper, and start to think not just about labelling yourself as creative, but making creativity a part of your self-identity.

We all have a unique self-identity, which represents how we see ourselves in relation to others. Our self-identity incorporates our values, attitudes, competencies and many other variables that influence what makes us uniquely ourselves.

Jason sees himself as intuitive, conscientious and intelligent, but also thinks he is the type of guy who tends to be a bit shy in social situations.

As humans, we seek opportunities to reinforce our self-identity. We do this through our behaviour. For example, if Jason sees conscientiousness as a key part of his self-identity, he will put himself in situations that allow him to work very hard and diligently.

As well as having these general views of ourselves, every individual has what psychologists call a 'creative self-identity'. This refers to whether we see ourselves as creative people, and whether this is a key part of who we are.

A large amount of research has shown that people who consider creativity a key part of their overall self-identity will engage in creative behaviours much more than people who don't consider themselves creative.

If Jason feels creativity is a key part of his self identity, he will seek out ways to reinforce this perception. For example, he will look for and complete tasks that require him to think creatively.

Research conducted by Kimberley Jaussi and her colleagues found that people who had high creative self-identities performed significantly more creatively at work. This relationship was even stronger when the individual had high creative self-efficacy — that is, they thought of themselves as being good at tasks which required creative thought.

Creative self-identity is a relatively easy dimension to measure. It can be done by asking someone if they agree with statements (as used in Jaussi's study) such as:

- In general, my creativity is an important part of my self image.
- My creativity is an important part of who I am.
- Overall, my creativity has little to do with how I feel about myself.
- My ability to be creative is an important reflection of who I am.

As well as being easy to measure, it can also be fairly malleable. If someone wants to increase their creative self-identity, they should seek opportunities to perform creatively.

For individuals:

- Seek out opportunities to think creatively. This might include taking an art class or getting involved in a work project that requires creative thinking.
- At the end of every day, write down at least one creative idea you had.

For organisations:

- If you are looking for people who can think creatively, screen applicants in the recruitment process with the creative self-identity questions mentioned above.
- Provide training in problem-solving and idea-generation techniques to maximise employees' performance on creative tasks.
- Managers should give staff members who do not have strong creative personal identities a lot of opportunities to think creatively to help them build a strong creative personal identity.

18

One of a kind

BROADLY SPEAKING, there are two different types of cultures we can create in a group: individualist and collectivist. Individualist cultures emphasise individual autonomy and uniqueness, prioritising personal goals over group goals and defining oneself as an individual as opposed to a member of a group. Collectivist cultures emphasise group harmony, prioritising group goals over individual ones and defining oneself in terms of the group one belongs to.

Amy's organisation has a collectivist culture. Most teams have a very high level of group cohesion. Getting along with co-workers and having harmonious working relationships is highly valued. Any type of conflict is strongly discouraged.

Unfortunately, the collectivist culture at Amy's work leads to a decrease in creativity. Research has found that individualist cultures are much more conducive to creative thought because they promote uniqueness and autonomy. Working in a group with a collectivist culture reduces creativity. One example is the way brainstorming groups are told they should never say no (see Chapter 33: Brainstorming is bollocks). Instead, the group tends to engage in 'groupthink', where people start to think in the same way and agree with each other the majority of the time to maintain harmony.

Most organisations do not encourage conflict; certainly not when working with a team of people. So when we break out into smaller groups for the purposes of creative thinking, we unconsciously try to satisfy the norms of the group. In practice, this means not putting forward ideas that seem 'a bit too crazy', trying to fulfil the needs of the group and not wanting to challenge the group for fear of disrupting it.

Angela Lee and her colleagues at Northwestern and Stanford Universities conducted a study to examine how individualism affects the way small groups generate ideas. The researchers divided participants into two groups. One group was primed to think individualistically by asking participants to write three statements about themselves, including how they felt they were different to most people and why they thought it was advantageous to stand out from the crowd. The second group was primed to think collectively — they had to write down three statements describing the group to which they belonged, why they felt they were like most other people and why they felt it was advantageous to blend in.

The researchers found that the individualist group produced more ideas and more creative ideas, supporting the notion that an individualist culture increases creativity.

For individuals:

- Whenever you are trying to think creatively, spend a few minutes prior to the task considering your unique qualities as an individual and what makes you different from your peers.

 For organisations:

- Encourage employees to think of themselves as individuals with unique qualities that set them apart from everyone else in the organisation. This can be done directly, by giving employees visualisation exercises which focus attention on their uniqueness, or informally, by frequently mentioning the notion that the organisation is made up of unique people who all bring something different to the company.

19

Why facilitation should be mandatory

A MY HAS PARTICIPATED IN many different work-shops over the past few years. What she is most anxious about is the personality mix of her small breakout group. Over the years, Amy has spent many workshops sitting with a group of outspoken, domi-nating people who left her too scared to disagree with them. She just wanted to maintain harmony in the group and agree with their suggestions, however uninspiring she thought they were.

These breakout groups never had a group leader or facilitator, so inevitably the dominant people would gain power and other group members would try to be amiable and agree with their suggestions.

As emphasised in the previous chapter, promoting an individualist culture is critical in helping people think more creatively. However, the natural behaviour of many groups is to act collectively.

One way of breaking this deadlock is to have a group facilitator for every idea-generation or creative-thinking session. When a group is facilitated, the need to conform drops significantly. Because someone is facilitating, you don't have to think as much about the group needs and are not as sensitive to group norms.

Amy has always felt much more comfortable participating in facilitated groups. She is able to stop focusing on pleasing the group and feel confident in putting forward her ideas because she knows that they will be heard.

Facilitation is an art and many books have focused on the skills of being a great facilitator. There is far too much to cover here, but I will leave you with just three tips for group facilitation.

First, go with the energy. If someone contributes a thought or idea to the group which provokes a lot of talking, you should keep the group focused on fleshing out and developing that energy-inspiring idea.

Second, it is your job to probe. Ask questions to gain depth around thoughts and ideas. For example, 'How does it achieve X?', 'What format would we sell it in?', 'Which consumer need does this idea meet?'

Finally, make sure you flesh out one idea before moving to the next. This is easier said than done because often, one idea will stimulate another. Try to be disciplined and keep the group on track to flesh out one idea before getting sidetracked to another one. Doing this will greatly improve the quality of your idea output.

☇ For individuals:

- When discussing ideas with your team or a small group of people, assign one of the people to facilitate the meeting.

For organisations:

- Whenever undertaking small group idea generation work, assign a facilitator to promote an individualist culture and increase creative output. This is particularly important in big idea generation sessions in which the wider group of people is broken into smaller groups. It is critical that each of the smaller groups has a facilitator to reduce groupthink and increase creativity.

20

Bigger isn't always better

TEAMS COME IN ALL DIFFERENT shapes and sizes, from pairs to departments of thirty or more. Fred has had the opportunity of working with a large number of different-sized teams. Early in his career, he tended to be placed in smaller teams of two to four people. He found those teams were creative and effective for the first few months of being together, but after this initial period, ideas became stale and repetitive.

Fred once worked in a team of over twelve people. He found this group quite difficult to work in — working with so many people made him feel like just one of many, or even anonymous. He noticed that other members of the team felt the same way, and because of this, they only made small contributions to team projects.

More recently, Fred worked with a medium-sized team of seven people. He found this team generated much greater creativity and innovation. Team members had enough brains and experience to generate a wide range of ideas. Yet it wasn't so large a group that he felt like a number, as opposed to a member.

When organisations structure and create teams, creativity is generally the last thing they're thinking about. However, recent research suggests that the size of teams is strongly linked to how innovatively an organisation will perform.

A group of researchers at the University of Oklahoma tried to find out the optimal size for teams that needed to think creatively. They found that organisations which were full of very large teams, more than fifteen members, were less creative than those made up of medium-sized teams of around six to nine members. The organisations made up of medium-sized teams were also more creative than those comprising smaller teams of five people or fewer.

🚶 For individuals:

- If you need to solve problems creatively and work with particularly large teams, speak to your boss about whether all team members are absolutely necessary, particularly at the idea-generation stage.
- If you tend to work on innovation projects in teams of fewer than five people, ask that more people be added to the team to increase creativity.

👫 For organisations:

- Consider the size of teams in your organisation, particularly those teams that are specifically formed to work on innovation projects. Ensure these teams are the right size to maximise both their creativity and that of the whole organisation.

21

Try to get along, but not too well

AFTER CONSIDERING THE SIZE of your team, always think about how well the team members get on with each other. Is the team constantly harmonious and never in conflict? Or are there often disagreements?

Amy's organisation encourages harmony and avoids conflict at all costs. As a result, her team tends to operate cohesively. It is rare for a team member to disagree or express disapproval at something suggested by another team member.

Teams that always try to minimise conflict tend to perform poorly on innovation projects. Because they are trying to please each other and not wanting to overstep any boundaries, team members do not take risks or challenge ideas. Furthermore, in cooperative environments, individuals become more aware of their similarities with other members of their team. As a consequence, they perceive themselves as part of a group and not as an independent, individual person.

This mindset encourages individuals to maintain harmony with other members of their group. To maintain harmony, they act cautiously and strive to avoid errors.

Researchers have found that a low-to-medium level of team cohesion is ideal for a creative culture. Teams that get along too well — that is, are highly cohesive — tend to fall victim to the 'not invented here' syndrome. That is, they discount ideas that were not born from within their team and do not look outside for stimulus, as opposed to being open to ideas and thoughts that lie outside their team.

Don't feel too concerned if there is occasionally some conflict within your team. A bit of conflict should be encouraged to ensure all points of view are heard and considered. Just be sure to manage this process carefully so that conflict is handled in a constructive way rather than experienced as a hostile or personal attack.

🚶 For individuals:

- There are ways to help your team become more comfortable engaging in a healthy level of conflict. Set up an overt code of conduct that allows for disagreements. This will make team members more comfortable with the idea of conflict and challenging each other, which will lead to more creative performances.

👫 For organisations:

- Be wary of rewarding teams that are overly cohesive, as chances are they are not producing innovative solutions to problems. Instead, openly encourage a moderate level of conflict so that the organisational culture becomes one in which people feel comfortable challenging each other and thus delivering more creative solutions to problems.

22

Fast-tracking intimacy

CHAPTER 22

H OW COMFORTABLE DO YOU feel with the people
you work with? Do you feel they will accept whatever you say or do you tend to censor your thoughts
and contributions?

Over the years, Emma experienced varying
degrees of comfort with the teams she worked with.
In general, the longer she was with a team, the more
comfortable she felt.

Feeling slightly uncomfortable within your workgroup is normal, particularly in the first few months
of working with a new team. Unfortunately, when we
feel uncomfortable with a group of people, we are less
creative. Creativity involves taking a risk; when we
feel uncomfortable, we don't want to take any risks in
front of the group for fear of embarrassing ourselves.

However, all is not lost if you belong to a newly
formed team or feel uncomfortable in your current
group. There are ways of accelerating the comfort you
feel with your team.

A study published in *Leadership Quarterly* set out to examine ways a group could rapidly increase its comfort level. In particular, the researchers were interested in the effect of experiencing an unusual or unexpected event at the start of a meeting and the effect this would have on the group dynamics.

The researchers found that strange or unconventional events caused the group of people who experienced them to feel a stronger attachment to each other. A shared experience increases comfort and honesty, which in turn enhances creativity.

For individuals:

- To increase the comfort level between yourself and a new team, suggest a team outing to an unusual event, such as a circus.

For organisations:

- If you need a team to think creatively, it is critical to fast-track team bonding and establish high levels of comfort. Organising unusual events for new teams could accelerate team comfort levels. For example, you could arrange a Gorilla Gram for their next team meeting.

23

When a hot date isn't just a pretty face

WHEN IT COMES TIME TO MATE, male bower-birds spend much of their time making colourful and elaborate nests. They use moss, sticks, leaves, grass and flowers and even paint the nest using berries. When selecting a mate, a female bowerbird is attracted to the males that have built the most creatively decorated nests.

A group of researchers from the University of Arizona hypothesised a similar link between mating and creativity among humans. In a series of experiments, participants were required to complete several creativity tasks. One group launched straight into the tasks while another group was asked to imagine themselves on a hot date with a top-quality mate. Those assigned to the 'hot date' group performed significantly better on the creativity tasks.

Interestingly, the tendency to be more creative after imagining oneself on a date with a physically attractive person was especially pronounced in males.

This tendency also applies to females, provided they imagine a person who is also trustworthy and reliable.

The researchers suggested that humans evolved in a way that required them to demonstrate their creativity to attract members of the opposite sex. Throughout history, creativity has been regarded as a sign of a person's adaptability and problem solving skills, which in turn suggest an ability to rise to the complex challenges of life — a valued characteristic in a mate.

Research from the University of Newcastle (UK) took the link between attracting the opposite sex and creativity a step further. They conducted a study which compared the sexual behaviour of 'creative types', such as artists and poets, to those who were in less creative professions. They found that creative types had sex more often than their non-creative counterparts. On average, 'creatives' had between four to ten sexual partners in their lives while 'non-creatives' had an average of three.

 For individuals:

- Before your next idea generation session, take a few minutes to imagine yourself at a romantic candlelit dinner for two with Angelina Jolie or George Clooney.

For organisations:

- Encourage employees to daydream about being on a romantic date before you need them to engage in a task that requires creative thought. You might want to make the task easier for them by plastering images of Hollywood sex symbols around the office.

24

Dastardly deadlines

IN OVERTLY CREATIVE INDUSTRIES, such as advertising and design, clients require staff members to generate ideas at a high speed. For example, the agency may be given just one week to develop a breakthrough campaign idea that is expected to capture the hearts and minds of an entire nation. A week may seem like a long time to some people, but the teams working on the breakthrough idea probably have another twelve projects with equally tight deadlines sitting on their desks.

At her agency, Emma frequently finds herself working to unrealistically tight deadlines. She is always baffled (and stressed) by the conditions under which agencies are required to think creatively. And Emma certainly does not envy the positions the idea generators, namely copywriters and art directors, are put under.

Rather than simply remaining baffled like Emma, Teresa Amabile from Harvard University decided to examine the relationship between deadlines and people's ability to think creatively.

She asked people to keep workplace diaries over a period of time. One of the things she asked people to record was deadlines for creative tasks, how this made them feel and the effect this had on their task performance.

She found that time pressure was a huge downer of creative thinking ability. People were unable to engage deeply with the problem or task required, which is necessary for solid creative thought to occur.

In addition, Amabile noted that creative tasks required a period of incubation in which the unconscious mind was free to digest the problem and start thinking of lateral but effective solutions. A tight deadline diminishes or entirely cuts off incubation time, which decreases a person's ability to think creatively about a problem.

Perhaps not surprisingly, Amabile discovered that people suffered from a time pressure hangover. People were less creative on deadline day and also for up to two days later.

If a deadline is unavoidable, a way to help counteract its effects is to ensure the people affected understand the reason for the urgency. This won't help them gain more incubation time, or time to engage more deeply with the problem. However, it will make them less frustrated, which allows the creative juices to flow slightly more freely.

🚶 For individuals:

- Educate your clients and manager about the effect of time pressure on creativity. Explain to them that creative output will be compromised if they insist on setting tight deadlines. Encourage them to consider extending deadlines or briefing you much earlier on jobs requiring creativity.

🚶 *For organisations:*

- Engage in better planning around deadlines for tasks that require creativity. Try to brief projects in earlier to ensure the team has the maximum amount of time possible to generate breakthrough ideas.
- If you do have to impose tight deadlines, make sure the team understands why the deadline was unavoidable to help counteract the negative effects of time pressure.

25

Chill out

JASON CONSIDERS HIMSELF highly strung. Getting stuck in peak hour traffic makes him want to pull his hair out and a lukewarm morning coffee makes him want to scream.

Unfortunately for Jason, his uptight nature is not doing his creative ability any favours. Research has indicated that being stressed or anxious is a creativity killer. Evolutionary psychologists believe that human beings developed emotions, in part, to change the way we think. In particular, anxiety causes us to narrow our attention so we can focus our efforts toward avoiding a potential threat.

Relaxation, the opposite of anxiety, widens our focus and increases our ability to digest large amounts of information and use this to solve the problem at hand. Researchers Nicola Baumann and Julius Kuhl found that relaxation helps us get in touch with our intuitive side. Intuition is crucial for creative thought because it can connect distant, unrelated concepts and reduce the boundaries and rigidity associated with anxiety.

In their study, Baumann and Kuhl presented people with a series of 'word triads' that were similar in theme. For instance, words like ice-cream, chocolate and dessert would be considered consistent. Words like fish, airplane, and golf would be considered inconsistent. The researchers flashed word triads on the screen in quick bursts and asked participants whether they were inconsistent or consistent. Participants also completed a survey which measured the extent to which they were able to relax and keep their stress under control. It was found that people who were better at relaxing were more successful at discriminating between the word triads. This is because they were able to access the intuitive part of their brains.

The researchers concluded that employees would be more intuitive, thus more creative, if they worked in a more relaxed setting.

 For individuals:

- Participate in a meditation or yoga class before or after work.
- If you find yourself feeling stressed or anxious, take a five-minute break and go for a walk outside to help relax.
- Before embarking on an activity that requires creative thinking, spend some time doing a relaxation exercise.

For organisations:

- Set up lunchtime classes to teach employees ways to relax.
- Encourage employees to take lunch breaks and morning and afternoon tea breaks to help them de-stress from the day's activities.

26
Mixed emotions

W E FEEL CERTAIN EMOTIONS in response to events that happen in our lives. A promotion or pay rise tends to make us feel good; being dumped by a partner feels bad. Sometimes, events make us feel a mix of emotions; both happy and sad at the same time.

Fred has often experienced mixed feelings. For example, when he graduated from university, he felt a huge sense of pride and achievement but he was also a little sad when he thought of having to leave behind his university days. His girlfriend often drags him along to romantic comedies that are funny but also quite touching (not that he would admit this to his mates).

Psychologists call mixed emotions ambivalence — the simultaneous mix of positive and negative feelings. Interestingly, researchers have found that our capacity to uncover creative, novel and effective solutions improves after we reflect on an event that provokes mixed feelings.

Christina Fong from the University of Washington divided people into four different emotion groups. One group was primed to feel happy, another to feel sad. A third group was primed to feel ambivalent while a control group was left emotionally neutral. After spending time in these emotional states, participants had to complete a creative-thinking task. People who were made to feel ambivalent performed significantly better on the task than any of the other three groups.

When we experience ambivalence, our brains sense that our environment is unusual. To accommodate this, our minds have evolved to think more creatively. In particular, we become more inclined to combine and integrate diverse concepts and thoughts, thus promoting more original insights.

🚶 *For individuals:*

- Try to recall instances in your life that promoted both joy and sadness, such as leaving home. Reflect on these ambivalent experiences for a few minutes before undertaking a task that requires creative thought.

🚶🚶 *For organisations*

- Instruct managers to spend some time at the beginning of meetings that require creative thought asking people to remember a time when they felt ambivalent. Remembering this event will help prime them to think creatively.

Brains also need support

ONE OF THE MOST FREQUENTLY researched areas in the field of creativity and innovation is the effect of management support. Studies have consistently shown that internal support for creativity significantly improves the creative performance of employees.

The management team at Fred's work actively supports creativity. The company sets aside resources for generating and implementing ideas, and encourages risk taking. At Fred's last workplace, the management team talked a lot about innovation and creativity, but never actually did anything about it. Experimentation and failure were not encouraged; Fred would go so far as to say they were frowned upon.

There are a number of elements to management support. The first point to note is that it needs to come from the top. It is much easier to achieve a creative workforce if the most senior people in the organisation genuinely and actively support and encourage creativity and innovation. Clients I have worked with where the boards encourage innovation have a lot more support for creativity across the organisation.

In addition, supervisors need to demonstrate support for creativity to their staff. Managers must be supportive of new and innovative ideas, otherwise those below will not be particularly motivated to come up with them.

 For organisations:

- There are three specific ways in which managers can demonstrate support for creativity:
  - Encourage risk taking and idea generation. People are more likely to produce original and creative solutions if they are given permission to do so.
  - Deliver feedback in a way that supports creativity. If managers are perceived to be highly critical of ideas and suggestions, this will reduce employees' motivation and ability to be creative. Fair, constructive and supportive feedback helps foster creativity.
  - Recognise employees' creative efforts, as discussed in Chapter 14. This may involve implementing a formal recognition program, or simply giving employees who come up with ideas a regular pat on the back.

28

Lead the way

T OP-LEVEL MANAGERS' LEADERSHIP style is one of
the biggest predictors and influencers of creativity
and innovation. At Amy's work, the senior management team tends to be fairly short-term focused in its
goals. Amy isn't 100% certain what their vision is for
the company, although she assumes one must exist.
Management lacks transparency about its plans for
the organisation. Amy often feels as if she is the last to
know when major changes occur. Overall, she thinks
her management team leaves a bit to be desired.

Dongil Jung from San Diego State University
and his colleagues set out to examine which style
of leadership was most conducive to creativity. He
examined CEOs' leadership styles across thirty-two
different companies.

Jung found that CEOs who had a 'transformational leadership' style had the most significant impact
on organisational innovation. Transformational leaders
tend to emphasise long-term goals and vision-based

CHAPTER 28

missions. Focusing on long-term goals over short-term outcomes helps direct employee efforts toward innovations that deliver long-term growth for the organisation. Companies with transformational leaders obtained significantly more patents than those with CEOs who had other styles of leadership.

Transformational leaders view organisational culture as a key source of employee influence. They tend to create cultures that support creativity and intellectual stimulation, which in turn impacts positively on organisational innovation. When staff believe the organisation supports innovation and creativity, innovation outcomes are greater.

Finally, because transformational leaders see value in creativity, they tend to put in place reward and recognition systems which intrinsically and extrinsically motivate employees to think creatively and laterally.

 For organisations:

- Use Avolio's transformational leadership test to measure how senior managers perform on this dimension. This test will also highlight areas for improvement to refine the leaders' management styles so they foster innovation and creativity.

Sleep on it

HAVE YOU EVER BEEN ADVISED to sleep on it? Emma hears this phrase every now and then and also gets advised to give a problem or decision 'the overnight test'.

These common phrases in our workplace lingo offer excellent advice for increasing our creativity. They refer to leaving your unconscious mind — that part of your brain that processes information outside of your conscious awareness — to sit and think about a problem.

The benefits of the unconscious mind have been brought very much into the mainstream through books such as *Blink* by Malcolm Gladwell. Gladwell talks about the power of the unconscious mind in making better decisions. In addition to being excellent for decision making, the unconscious mind can help us think more creatively.

To set the record straight, the unconscious mind is not some magical entity, although it is rather amazing, and it is not in the least bit airy-fairy. Thousands of scientific studies have explored how it works and why it's so powerful.

There are two things that you should know about the unconscious mind. First, it is goal-directed. Studies have shown that when you have a goal and give yourself time to process it — that is, give it time to sit in your head, uninterrupted — the unconscious mind will work hard to find a solution. Indeed, the more time you give it, the better the result. These studies also found that when there was no clear goal specified for the unconscious mind to work toward, it did not do a lot of processing.

You might want to set your unconscious mind the goal of solving problems through creative thinking. For example, you might want to get it processing on goals such as 'How can we promote product X?' or 'How can we double our profits this financial year?'

The other great thing about the unconscious mind is its ability to process and store a vast amount of information. This is in contrast to the conscious mind, which can only process seven or eight bits of information at once. The unconscious mind's large processing and storage capacity is one of the main reasons it's so effective at creative thinking. It has access to a huge amount of information and the capacity to know which pieces to focus on and which to ignore.

Here is one way to use your unconscious mind in a particularly efficient manner — once you are familiar with the problem to be solved, direct your attention to something entirely different. Studies have shown that distracting the unconscious mind for five to ten minutes is long enough for it to start coming up with some solutions. The unconscious mind will immediately get to work making strange and unexpected connections that your rational, conscious mind could never come up with.

The beauty of using your unconscious mind for creativity is that it can work away on the problem in the background while your conscious mind is attending to other things.

🚶 *For individuals:*

- When facing a problem that requires creative thinking, try to not think about the problem for a day and see what your unconscious mind spits out (sometimes at the most unusual times).
- When running meetings or workshops that require creative thinking, brief attendees on the problem the day before to give their unconscious minds some time to start tackling it.

🚶🚶 *For organisations:*

- Give employees plenty of time to solve problems that require creative thought.

30

Sorry to interrupt you, but…

CHAPTER 30

DURING OUR DAY-TO-DAY TASKS, we are often interrupted by formal office procedures or colleagues who want a chat. These interruptions are often unwelcome because we feel our work is being impeded.

Amy gets very frustrated when a colleague interrupts her work to discuss last night's reality TV show episode. However, Amy's colleagues are actually doing her a favour; interrupting the day-to-day grind enhances creative thinking.

At work, we often complete routine tasks without much thought or social interaction. When an interruption occurs, the person's attention is switched in the direction of the interruption. This interruption makes the individual take a step back from the task, which then enables it to be seen in a different light upon return. The change of perspective can be very effective at increasing creative problem solving abilities.

Gerardo Okhuysen from the University of Utah gave a problem solving task to 168 people in forty-two four-person groups. While completing the task, a researcher interrupted half of the groups, instructing them to complete a task that did not directly relate to the problem they were solving.

Okhuysen found that the formal interruption helped the groups take a step back from the problem, and as a result, come up with more solutions than the groups who were not interrupted. Interestingly, Okhuysen found that groups who were more familiar with each other interrupted themselves naturally and did not need formal interruptions.

Be aware, of course, that constant disruptions are different from the occasional, planned interruption and can be disruptive instead of constructive.

For individuals:

- Schedule formal interruptions when you need to think creatively about a problem. For example, ask a co-worker to come into the room to discuss an unrelated topic once every hour.

For organisations:

- Encourage employees to interrupt each other when they are completing tasks which require creative thinking.

31

Rubbish in, rubbish out

THINK ABOUT WHAT HAPPENS when you learn something new that applies to your work. Is there a process for sharing this information with peers and storing it? Is there a formal way to access this information at a later date? And finally, how effectively is this knowledge used to drive creativity and organisational innovations?

The answers to those questions should give you a pretty good idea of how advanced your company's knowledge management is.

Fred comes across a lot of information in his day to day job. He often visits trend-spotting and consumer behaviour websites to find out what influences his chocolate-loving consumers. However, the information Fred reads generally goes in one eye and out the other.

Knowledge management and its relationship to organisational innovation have become increasingly popular areas of research. Many academics have explored the link between innovation and the way organisations manage and share knowledge.

Research by Meriam Ismail from the Private Education Department in Malaysia demonstrated that the way an organisation prioritises learning and knowledge management has an enormous impact on innovation. In some organisations, knowledge management had an even greater impact on innovation than having a 'creative culture' — one which was challenging, open and trusting and gave staff members time to generate ideas.

Organisations' learning structures must take into account three key areas to ensure successful innovation through managing of knowledge and information. These three areas are:

- Creating knowledge and learning.
- Sharing and transferring this knowledge.
- Implementing the knowledge.

The first stage, knowledge creation, must be exploratory to maximise the breadth of learning and potential for innovation. If the knowledge creation process only confirms what you already know, you will have missed a major opportunity to expand your knowledge base.

When it comes to knowledge sharing, organisations need both formal and informal methods. For example, some organisations employ a team of people to manage all knowledge through an intranet or shared folder. Other companies try to enforce regular information sharing sessions with peers.

Finally, challenge yourself to use this knowledge as stimulus for projects that require creative thought and an understanding of the broader context. If you don't apply the knowledge to future projects, the previous two steps have been a waste.

For individuals:

- Challenge yourself to bring as much relevant and interesting knowledge into the organisation as you can. After finding this knowledge, make sure you share it with your team and the wider organisation, if possible.
- If systems for sharing don't already exist, try to create some. For example, ask IT to create a section on the company intranet or set up a folder where knowledge can be catalogued and stored for future reference. You could even send around a weekly email updating employees on new knowledge that has been added to the system.
- Organise weekly or fortnightly information-sharing sessions with your team to have a show and tell of new information learned.

For organisations:

- Ensure employees are assessed on continuous learning, including how successfully they share and apply these learnings.
- Mentoring can be an effective means of passing knowledge down the ranks. A less popular but just as effective technique is 'reverse mentoring'. Firms such as design consultancy IDEO have adopted this technique, in which senior employees are paired with junior employees as their mentors. This allows the senior person to keep in touch with what younger employees are experiencing, such as Generation Y trends that could lead to important product or service innovations.
- Set up a system on the company intranet for employees to post and categorise knowledge to make it easy for the rest of the company to access it when needed.

32

Taking off the blinkers

BROADENING YOUR KNOWLEDGE and experience is an effective way to increase creativity, as discussed in Chapter 5. The more places we look, the more thoughts are likely to be triggered, which increases our ability to think creatively. Jason finds it much easier to think creatively when he purposefully exposes himself to new and varied information.

Richard Friedman from the University of Maryland and several of his colleagues took this finding a step further to see if the facial expressions associated with widening and narrowing our visual perception affected creativity.

Friedman and his colleagues thought a simple bodily cue of broadening your attention, such as raising your eyebrows, could increase performance on a creative thinking task. Likewise, they thought furrowing your brows, an act associated with narrowing your attention, would have the opposite effect on creativity.

Participants were divided into two groups: one eyebrow raising and one eyebrow furrowing. For two minutes, participants were required to hold their respective facial expressions while completing a creative thinking task: generating as many uses as possible for a pair of scissors.

Upon completion of the task, all ideas were scored on originality and quantity. The eyebrow-raising, attention-broadening group generated significantly more original ideas and a greater quantity of ideas.

 ### For individuals:

- Try to raise your eyebrows for several minutes while completing a task that requires creative thought.
- Avoid furrowing your brows when you are in a situation that requires creative thinking.

 ### For organisations:

- As an exercise at the beginning of workshops and meetings, ask participants to try to raise their eyebrows for a few minutes, and to do this again when they are completing tasks that require creativity.

Brainstorming is bollocks

I F YOU ARE READING THIS BOOK, chances are you're familiar with the rules of brainstorming: no idea is a bad idea; don't say 'no', say 'maybe'; and so on. While these are great rules in theory, in practice they are not particularly useful. This is because people communicate as much in non-verbal form as they do with words. While people may say 'maybe' in their words, their crossed arms and furrowed brows are saying 'no' loudly and clearly.

This kind of behaviour is enough to put off even the most confident idea generator. And those who are less confident may decide that it's wiser never to open their mouths. Fred has certainly felt inhibited from speaking during poorly facilitated brainstorms.

The other thing to note is that not everyone generates ideas most effectively in a group. Amy, for example, actually does her best work on her own, yet such people are often forgotten about in creativity workshops.

Robert Epstein from Harvard University developed a technique called 'shifting', which overcomes both of these problems and significantly increases the number of ideas generated in group work, either in casual meetings or more formal workshops.

Shifting combines individual and group idea generation. The technique begins with people generating ideas individually for about five minutes. Then they merge into groups for five minutes, and listen to, and build on, the ideas they have generated individually. Following this five minutes, the participants go back to working individually for five minutes, then repeat the group idea-building process for a final five minutes. So to summarise:

- Five minutes spent generating ideas individually.
- Five minutes spent as a group, building on the individually generated ideas.
- Another five minutes individually generating ideas.
- A final five minutes building on these new individually generated ideas.

Epstein compared the results of this technique to a group of people brainstorming together for twenty minutes, with no individual work. He found that the group that employed the shifting technique generated significantly more and significantly broader ideas.

This technique should provide some hope to those who struggle in group idea-generation sessions. Individual idea generation is powerful and important. This technique should also hopefully encourage individuals, once they have some ideas, to discuss these ideas with friends or colleagues and allow them to grow and be built upon.

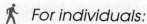 *For individuals:*

- Use the shifting technique in any workshops or meetings you run that require creative thought.
- Whenever you are generating ideas individually, always find a friend or colleague to bounce the idea off and enable your idea to grow.

For organisations:

- Use the shifting technique in every meeting or workshop where the aim is to generate a wide range of ideas or solutions. This technique gives the more introverted people the chance to be heard and dramatically increases the number and quality of ideas these sessions will generate.

34

Why left can be right

Like all human beings, every time Jason moves his body, his brain lights up with activity. Neuroscientists have argued that if we can activate certain parts of our brains, it can make other parts of the brain light up as well.

Activities involving the left-hand side of our bodies activate the right hemisphere of our brains and vice versa. The right hemisphere is thought to contain the area of intuition and insight which allows the individual to be holistic and creative. In left-handed or ambidextrous people, the functions might be reversed or differently configured. Studies have not yet clarified this however.

Nicola Baumann and her colleagues decided to explore a method that people could use to deliberately activate the right-hand side of their brains. They divided participants into two groups. One group had to squeeze a ball with their left hands while the other group had to squeeze a ball with their right hands.

Participants then had to undergo a series of tasks to determine whether the ball squeezing activated different regions of the brain.

The researchers found that squeezing a ball with one hand activated the opposite side of the brain. People who squeezed the ball with their left hands activated the right hemispheres in their brains, and vice versa for the right hand.

Baumann and her fellow researchers noted that when participants activated their right hemispheres, this activation spread to several areas. Specifically, they found that squeezing a ball in the left hand activated a brain circuit associated with thinking holistically and intuitively, and thus more creatively.

🏃 *For individuals:*
- Before undertaking a task that requires creative thought, squeeze your left hand for a couple of minutes.

👫 *For organisations:*
- Encourage employees to squeeze their left hands prior to creative thinking tasks, meetings and workshops.

35

I like you, but can I trust you?

CHAPTER 35

To FOSTER CREATIVITY IN AN organisation, it is important for managers to recruit people they feel they can trust. While this may sound obvious, it is quite rare for managers to consciously take this variable into account. Most recruitment and selection processes tend to focus on ability, core competencies and previous work experience.

Research has shown that managers who trust their staff are more likely to encourage them to be creative, which in turn is critical to people's ability to perform creatively at work.

Fred experienced both sides of this issue with his last two bosses. Thanks to his exceptional performance on a couple of key projects, Fred's current boss Larry trusts him completely and implicitly. As a result, Larry gives Fred a lot of room to move with the tasks he sets and encourages Fred to think creatively in relation to these projects.

In contrast, Fred's previous boss didn't trust anyone. She rarely gave Fred or his co-workers any challenging work to do or the freedom to think creatively. As a result, Fred did not contribute much in the way of creative thought to the projects he was assigned to and instead, simply went through the motions.

As well as managers trusting their staff, it is critical for people within teams and organisations to trust each other. Proposing a creative idea can be difficult for many employees because they feel their ideas will be ridiculed or rejected. Employees who trust their employers are looking after the employees' best interests are much more inclined to offer ideas and engage in other innovative behaviours.

Chris Clegg and his colleagues from the University of Sheffield identified two different types of trust in organisations: *trust that is heard* and *trust that benefits*. *Trust that is heard* is the expectation that the organisation will take your ideas seriously. *Trust that benefits* is the belief that the organisation has your best interest at heart. This kind of trust is linked to how much people think they will be recognised for their input.

To examine the effect of trust on innovation Clegg and colleagues surveyed 128 design engineers from two large aerospace organisations. They found *trust that is heard* directly related to idea implementation. *Trust that benefits* influenced the number of ideas generated which in turn influenced the number of ideas implemented.

The researchers suggested that employees who trust their employers are more likely to think creatively at work because they feel the workplace is supportive of it.

For individuals:

- When deciding on whether you will accept a job at an organisation, or whether you will take up an opportunity to join a new team within your existing workplace, give some thought to whether you feel you can trust the people you will be working with. If you don't feel you can trust them in the areas that are important to you, you probably won't be doing your best work.
- For projects that require innovative thought, try to team up with people who you implicitly trust.

For organisations:

- During the recruitment process, always ask yourself if you think you can trust the job applicant. If the answer is no, you are better off not employing them.

36

Don't try to beat 'em; join 'em

WITHIN INDUSTRIES SUCH AS advertising, technology and finance, there is a belief that competition increases creativity. Emma's advertising agency often pits creative teams against each other to compete for who can generate the biggest and best idea for a project.

Research conducted by Teresa Amabile at Harvard University examined the effect of competition on creativity at work. She found that competition actually reduces creativity.

When people compete with each other, they are less likely to share information. No team wants to give away the upper hand, so information is closely guarded. Likewise, teams don't debate ideas and thoughts with each other because this might also help an opposing team win. Certainly, at Emma's workplace, teams who are competing against each other on a project rarely share ideas.

By contrast, when teams collaborate rather than compete, they share information much more freely.

This is particularly important because it is extremely rare for one person to have all the pieces of the puzzle. Instead, people with different knowledge bases and experiences all contribute elements which the group combines into a creative and effective solution.

In addition, when teams collaborate, people tend to feel comfortable sharing and debating thoughts. This debating process can be extremely powerful in shaping ideas and bringing them to life.

 ### For individuals:

- Avoid competition wherever possible.
- If your manager sets up competition between yourself and another team, ask if you can instead partner with the other team to achieve a better outcome.
- Seek to collaborate with others within and outside of your organisation to solve problems.

 ### For organisations:

- If you want people to perform creatively, avoid setting up competition.
- When you give the company a challenge, actively encourage people to collaborate in solving the problem.

Down with downsizing

L AST YEAR, A NEW CEO joined Amy's organisation. To help reverse the company's declining profits, the new CEO immediately retrenched a large percentage of the workforce including a couple of Amy's closest friends. This strategy helped the organisation appear to be more profitable in the short-term, but the CEO unknowingly affected the organisational drivers of creativity.

Teresa Amabile studied organisational downsizing and its impact on creativity with a Fortune 500 electronics company. After she had conducted some in-house research with the organisation on predictors of creative performance, the company announced it was planning an 18% reduction across its entire global workforce. Amabile immediately asked permission to go back into the company and examine first hand the effects of downsizing.

Every good scientist loves a control group, that is, a group which is not directly affected by the variable being measured. Scientists compare this group with the experimental group — the group being affected by the variable the scientists are studying. Amabile was lucky in this situation, because the downsizing in this organisation affected different departments in different ways — some were relatively unaffected and these unaffected departments served as the natural control group. Amabile was thus able to compare the effects of anticipated downsizing and actual downsizing across the organisation.

You may be surprised to learn that Amabile found the anticipation of the downsizing had a more severe effect than the downsizing itself. Once people started to hear about retrenchments and staff cuts, employees began to disengage with work tasks. Since task engagement is a key predictor of creativity, the anticipation of downsizing had an immediate negative impact on creativity within the workplace.

Once the downsizing occurred, Amabile then examined the difference in creativity between teams that had retained most of their members and those where the structure had changed significantly. As expected, the workgroups that experienced the greatest change showed the most significant reduction in creativity.

And the problem didn't end as soon as the downsizing had been completed. Creativity remained significantly down for four months following the downsizing.

𝕏 For individuals:

- If you hear rumours about your organisation downsizing, talk to your manager about the importance of transparency in the process. This could help reduce the anticipatory effects of downsizing.

For organisations:

- When going through downsizing, it is important to undertake additional strategies to maintain creativity, such as applying some of the findings in this book. Doing nothing will stifle creativity and innovation.
- Managers must maintain open and transparent communication with employees, especially those whose roles demand creativity, to help counter the negative effects of downsizing.

38

Stereotyping can be good

CHAPTER 38

FRED WORKS IN A female-dominated team. His
group occasionally gets called the 'emotionally in
touch' team, given the oversupply of females. Emotions
and feelings about people and events are one of the
regular topics of discussion and most team members
have a high level of self-awareness in these matters.
Fred is comfortable with expressing emotion and
quite enjoys the positive stereotype that his team has
acquired of being emotionally in touch.

Somewhat surprisingly, thinking about this stereotype has an impact on the creative performance
of Fred's team. Researchers have found that after
people consider the favourable stereotypes of their
groups — such as when male employees think about
the perception that their mathematical skills are more
advanced than women's — they tend to work more
rapidly and creatively but less carefully and accurately.

In contrast, after people are reminded of the
unfavourable stereotypes of their groups — such as

when male employees think about the perception that their verbal skills are less advanced than women's — they tend to work more carefully and accurately although less rapidly and creatively.

Some research in Germany conducted by Beate Seibt and Jens Forster suggested that after individuals were asked to think about the unfavourable stereotypes of their group, they become more focused on shortfalls and deficiencies. As a result, they strive to minimise errors and work cautiously.

On the other hand, after people consider the favourable stereotypes of their group, they become more focused on opportunities and aspirations. Rather than striving to minimise errors, they try to maximise gains and fulfil aspirations. They are, hence, more willing to accept risks, which fosters novel and creative suggestions.

 ### For individuals:

- To think creatively, spend some time reflecting on the favourable stereotypes of your workgroup. By doing so, you will become more focused on opportunities and aspirations, which increases creativity.

 ### For organisations:

- To ensure that employees work creatively, encourage them to specify the groups they belong to, such as female, engineer and finance. Then they should identify the favourable stereotypes of this group — such as the perception that engineers are intelligent. By undertaking this thought process, the group will increase its creative performance.

39

I did it my way

E MMA HAS HAD A VARIETY of managers. Some of them micromanaged her while others took a big step back and macro-managed. With a macro-manager, Emma felt a great deal more autonomous and empowered. Little did she know, this feeling did wonders for her creative ability.

Many creativity researchers have concluded there is a strong relationship between how independent a person feels and how creative they are. When people feel autonomous, they are more likely to engage in trial and error and find more effective ways of doing things.

Recently, Chantal Levesque and Luc Pelletier set out to examine just how sensitive this relationship was. The researchers split people up into two groups. The first group was asked to read several sentences which included words related to the concept of obligation, such as 'forced', 'pressured' and 'controlled'. A second group was asked to read sentences containing words that related to autonomy, such as 'absorbed', 'interested', 'delighted' and 'challenge'.

The researchers found that participants who read sentences about autonomy felt significantly more engaged in a task they had to complete afterward. When people feel more engaged and absorbed, they are more creative. The group that read sentences about obligation felt less motivated to complete the task.

Levesque and Pelletier also noted how easy it can be to prime people to feel independent. Indeed, simply asking people to read a few sentences relating to the concept is enough to provoke feelings of autonomy, which can increase their creativity.

 ### For individuals:

- Before undertaking a task that requires creative thinking, read over several sentences that relate to autonomy.
- Create your own word-find puzzle where you have to find words that relate to autonomy.

 ### For organisations:

- Ensure that managers lean toward macro-managing their employees to provide a workplace that offers autonomy.
- Help managers feel comfortable with delegating large amounts of responsibility to employees, to help them feel challenged and independent at work.

Cut up your tie

CHAPTER 40

THEY SAY CLOTHES MAKETH the man. They also maketh the creative thinker.

Consider the clothes you tend to wear to work and the official organisational dress code if there is one. Does your workplace tend to the casual side? In some organisations I have worked at, at least a quarter of the office wore 'flip flops' on any summer day. Other companies have required me to wear a suit, which made me feel uncomfortable and a bit ridiculous (I am not a suit person).

Amy's company requires that employees wear a suit to work (with an optional tie for men). However, every Friday is mufti day, when Amy and her co-workers can dress down in jeans and a nice t-shirt. Not surprisingly, employees look forward to Fridays, and not only because they signal the end of the working week.

Many of us choose outfits in the morning based on how we want to appear to the world (or meet the organisational dress code). But what we wear has a big impact on how we feel. Your clothing provides a signal of your personality to those around you. It also has a strong impact on internal attitudes and feelings, and thus the way your mind works.

When people wear formal outfits such as a suit and tie, they tend to feel conservative and restricted, metaphorically and physically. Wearing formal attire can make us feel as if we are playing a role — that of a conservative businessperson.

By contrast, when we wear casual and comfortable attire, we become more relaxed and start to feel at ease. There is no need or room for formalities when you are wearing jeans and thongs.

Not surprisingly, these feelings have a significant impact on creativity. Wearing casual attire increases our creativity. This occurs because we feel more relaxed and comfortable; states that are highly conducive to creativity and risk-taking.

For individuals:

- If your organisation does not have a casual dress code, speak to your boss about implementing some casual days, particularly when you will need to think creatively.

For organisations:

- If creative thinking and innovation are key to your business, consider making the dress code less formal.
- Allow employees who are in the creative thinking stages of a project to wear casual clothing.
- Allow employees to wear casual clothing for all creative-thinking and idea-generation workshops. You will find the outcomes much more creative and effective.

Why you shouldn't want it to be a team effort

THINK ABOUT YOUR TEAM'S most recent success. Now consider what you attributed that success to — was it the qualities of the team, for example, its cohesiveness and propensity for great team work? Or was success ascribed to the unique qualities of each individual in the group?

Fred's team recently got the green light on a new chocolate bar they developed. Fred thought of the success as a team effort. Fred and his colleagues had been working together for months on developing, researching and finally making the new chocolate bar. When it came to attributing success, Fred thought the project succeeded because the team worked so well together. Is Fred's perception helpful when it comes to thinking creatively?

This issue has been examined by Jack Goncalo at the University of California, Berkeley. Goncalo set up a study to explore the relationship between team innovativeness and to what the teams ascribed their successes.

From observing and measuring the behaviour of several teams, he found that after some teams succeed on a task, they tended to ascribe this achievement to qualities of the workgroup. For example, they might attribute their success to a sense of cohesion that pervades the team. As a consequence, such teams do not focus on the unique qualities of each individual. They become inclined to emphasise only the points of view and suggestions that most of the members of their team agree on, which tends to stifle originality and creativity.

In contrast, Goncalo found that after success, some teams ascribed their achievements to the qualities of each individual. For instance, they might attribute their success to the experience of one individual and the originality of another individual. These teams become more inclined to accept unique suggestions, which promote novelty, creativity and innovation.

Goncalo concluded that teams that perceive their successes as due to the unique qualities of individual members tend to perform more creatively.

 For individuals:

- For all team successes you are involved in, encourage the team to attribute success to the unique qualities of each team member. This will ensure the team remains innovative and stays open to unique ideas and suggestions proposed by individual team members.
- This exercise can also be done retrospectively. You can ask your teammates to identify previous instances when a lofty goal was achieved. The workgroup should convene and identify the unique qualities, skills, insights and contributions of each individual.

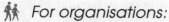 *For organisations:*

- When giving feedback to teams, frame the feedback around how each individual contributed to the success. Be sure to highlight the unique qualities of each individual that was instrumental to the success. Providing feedback in this way helps the team remain creative and innovative.

42

Talking in the abstract

WHEN PEOPLE ARE ASKED to come up with a new idea, more often than not they take the path of least resistance. This involves recalling very basic examples that relate to the problem and using those as a starting point.

Emma recently had to think of a new idea for a sales promotion of one of her client's latest breakfast cereals. She took the path of least resistance by thinking of an idea that had already been executed in the past (running a co-promotion with a blockbuster animated film, and altered that idea slightly to make it seem a little bit new — running a co-promotion with the sequel to that film). In other words, while the film was different, the idea was essentially the same. This thought process is not conducive to effective creative thinking.

Giving people abstract stimuli and setting problems related to abstract concepts have proven to be effective ways to stop people from taking the path of least resistance. The abstract stimulus should be related to the broader context in which the problem sits, such as local or global trends (e.g. consumers' desire for more environmentally-friendly products).

This method has been researched in several studies, including one experiment conducted at the University of Alabama. In this study, people were asked to imagine and describe what life forms might be like on other planets. One group was instructed to base its ideas for other life forms on specific earth animals. A second group was given more abstract instructions — to think about general environmental conditions and survival needs on other planets. Specifically, they were told to focus on 'higher order principles' associated with the ability to live and function, such as sensing conditions in their environment, protecting themselves from danger and reproducing. Finally, a control group was given no specific instructions on how to generate ideas for life forms on other planets.

A group of independent judges rated the novelty of each group's thoughts. Novelty ratings for the 'abstract' group were, on average, 58% higher than the 'specific' group, and also significantly higher than the control group.

The researchers explained that this exercise of considering the abstract forced participants to think broadly about the problem at hand and avoid drawing on specific examples from their past experience. The results showed that this approach led to a wider range and better quality of ideas.

This finding confirms the importance of the way in which a problem is worded and also the stimuli which are provided. Indeed, stimuli should be designed to provoke abstract thought around the greater context in which the problem sits.

For individuals:

- When solving a problem that requires creative thought, seek out stimuli that make you consider the bigger picture. If you are solving a problem for an airline, seek out macro consumer trends, decision-making trends and any trends surrounding the travel and tourism industry.

For organisations:

- Rather than providing people with specific, concrete instructions, give teams instructions that encourage them to think more abstractly and broadly about the problem. Providing people with stimuli such as macro trends can also help thinking become more abstract, which produces more novel solutions to problems.

43

Forward to the future

WHICH OF THE FOLLOWING two statements is most true of how you perform tasks at work?

(a) I am very focused on reaching my goals (big picture, future-oriented aspirations).
(b) I am very focused on fulfilling my obligations (smaller details, day-to-day practicalities).

If you had to describe the organisation in which you work, what statement fits best? Is there much variation between departments within the organisation?

If you chose (a) in response to the two options at the beginning of this chapter, chances are you are forward looking, focused on future goals and what psychologists call 'promotion focused'. Please note this term has nothing to do with getting moved up the hierarchy at work, as the name might suggest.

In contrast, if you chose (b) as being a more accurate self-description, you tend to focus more on rules and requirements, try to avoid making mistakes and are more 'prevention focused.'

Amy felt that as an individual, she was naturally more promotion focused. She thought herself to be very focused on setting and achieving future goals, looking ahead and not dwelling too much on the past. However, her organisation made her feel more prevention focused at work. Her manager never encouraged risk taking or set targets that required a sudden change in company growth. As a consequence, Amy was careful to do her job properly, take minimal risks and just do what was required to avoid making a mistake.

Research has shown that when we consider our current duties and obligations — that is, we are prevention focused — it reduces our creativity. We resort to traditional behaviours and avoid taking risks. Risk taking gets in the way of fulfilling our requirements. Because we are striving to minimise short-falls, we tend to engage in activities or think about solutions that have worked in the past. In other words, we resort to traditional behaviours and ideas.

When we think about goals, hopes and aspirations for the future — when we are promotion focused — our creativity increases. When we focus on these hopes and goals, we think about broad, abstract concepts rather than specific, concrete objects or activities. In this mode, we become much less detail oriented and are much more open to taking risks. We start thinking about what we could gain in the future, rather than how we can prevent losses in the present. Needless to say, having a promotion focus is a very effective way of increasing creativity.

The same principle also applies to CEOs' letters to shareholders. Researchers found that predicting a firm's innovation success can be as simple as analysing the words the company's CEO uses in these letters.

Rajesh Chandy and his colleagues from the University of Minnesota revealed that organisations whose CEO used more future-oriented, promotion-focused words in communication with shareholders performed significantly better at innovation. For example, these companies were shown to adopt new technology at a greater pace and develop innovations more quickly than their competitors.

Being prevention focused is very appropriate for some jobs, such as those that require careful analysis and attention to detail. However, having a promotion focus is much more conducive to jobs or tasks that require creative thinking and lateral solutions.

The good news is that every human being has the capacity to be aspiration-focused. However, only some people, those with high self-esteem, naturally tend to use it all the time. One of the most effective ways to activate a promotion focus is to take on more autonomy and responsibility. When your boss gives you challenging work and a large amount of responsibility over this work, you tend to feel more autonomous.

𝕏 For individuals:

- Before embarking on creative-thinking tasks, think about the status, recognition, and role you would like to receive one year from now if you generate a revolutionary and significant idea or solution.
- Think positively about the future and your hopes and aspirations before starting an activity that requires creative thinking.

👫 *For organisations:*

- Organisations in which success depends on creativity and innovation should foster a promotion-focused culture. Managers' language should reflect a promotion focus, rather than prevention focus. This will make employees feel more autonomous and promotion focused, which will lead to more creative behaviours.
- Managers need to give their staff a large degree of autonomy in tasks they are given, which will increase employees' promotion focus and will lead to a more creative solution on the assigned project.

Scrap the detail

THINK BACK TO SOME OF the tasks your boss has recently given you to complete. How much detail did the instructions contain? Did he or she simply set you an objective and leave the rest up to you, or did you get a step-by-step breakdown of exactly what needed to be done and how?

Jason is in the habit of providing a great deal of detail when he sets new tasks for his staff to complete, including a description of what he wants and how they should go about doing it. Essentially, Jason was leaving his staff with the task of robotically following his instructions.

If you have people reporting to you, take a moment to consider your style as a manager. Think about how you tend to brief your team on jobs. Do you trust your employees enough just to tell them what needs to be achieved? Or do you provide very detailed instructions how to go about it, so that in your mind, nothing can go wrong?

Sometimes it can be very tempting to provide details. It is a way of feeling in control of the project outcome and a way of avoiding potential complications in the future. After all, if an employee follows your specific instructions to the letter, how can the project fail?

Unfortunately, providing detailed instructions is a creativity killer. When we have specific instructions on how to complete a task, that is, we are given no autonomy, we are less creative. When given detailed instructions, our minds tend to shut down and we follow the step-by-step breakdown of what needs to be done. It is very unlikely that creative ideas will emerge from this behaviour.

By contrast, when we only receive the task objective, we feel as if we have much more autonomy. Having this autonomy promotes creative thinking.

For individuals:

- Be aware of the way in which people give you instructions. If you are given a task that requires a creative and lateral solution, ask your boss to simply tell you what needs to be achieved and assure him or her you will figure out how to do it or ask if you need help.
- For managers, when you have a task that requires creative thinking, be sure to give employees only the task objective, and let them figure out how to achieve it. If they need help, they can always speak to you, but by giving them open-ended instructions, you will enable them to feel autonomous and deliver a more creative solution.

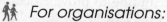 *For organisations:*

- Educate managers who set tasks which require creative thinking to be minimal with their instructions. Instead, coach them to give staff only the objective that needs to be achieved and any background information necessary to understand the task and its context.

45

I think therefore I can

WHAT DO LUDWIG VAN BEETHOVEN, Isaac Newton and Pablo Picasso have in common? They are all responsible for perpetuating the myth that there are only a small number of truly creative people in the world. This notion dissuades people from even attempting to be creative.

When I run workshops in creative thinking, I constantly come up against this myth. People often tell me that they are not very creative and never have been. If Emma was in one of my workshops, she would insist that the creative thinking be left to the other people in her team. The sad thing is that Emma and others feel this way because of how society defines creativity. Creativity, society implies, is something that is best left to the artistic community, the painters, actors and writers. The rest of us should just stick to our day jobs.

Self talk often gets in the way. Those of us who believe ourselves to be non-creative are constantly reinforcing this message in our brains. When faced with a task requiring creativity, we tell ourselves 'I am not creative'. These thoughts can be damaging as we begin to truly believe them, which prevents us from even trying out creative behaviours.

However, when you examine the neurology behind how ideas are formed, you will find that nothing could be further from the truth. Every human of average intelligence has the capacity to think creatively and come up with novel and useful ideas.

In our brains at any one time, we have millions of different thoughts floating around. An idea or new thought is born when two different thoughts compete for attention. Sometimes, to reconcile this competition, the brain can form these two disparate thoughts into a new idea.

With this scientific explanation in mind, it should be obvious that everyone has the capacity to be creative. But what's really important is that you start to believe this yourself. Research suggests that when you think you are creative, you think more creatively.

𝕏 For individuals:

- If you ever start self-talking about your lack of creative ability, stop. Think back to this explanation of how ideas are formed and remind yourself that you are creative and cannot help being this way even if you try.
- At the end of each day, write down at least one good idea you had, no matter how small it is.

𝕏𝕏 For organisations:

- Constantly reinforce the message that all employees are creative. The more this message is reinforced, the more likely it is that people will start to realise that they are creative and in response, act that way.

46

Inductrination

THE MAJORITY OF ORGANISATIONS Emma has
worked for had minimal induction processes. More
often that not, she was given a desk, a computer, a
phone and a password. If she was lucky, a co-worker
would show her where the bathrooms were.

Most people don't think the induction process is
particularly relevant to innovation. Helen Shipton and
several researchers from various business schools and
universities in the UK set out to test this proposition.

Their research found that a sophisticated and
extensive induction process was significantly related
to innovation performance. They suggested that a
comprehensive induction process gave individuals the
opportunity to notice performance gaps in the organisation and started their minds working on solving
those problems. This is particularly effective because
when people have just started their employment, they
are still objective and removed from organisational
processes.

In contrast, people who are not given extensive induction take much longer to identify gaps, by which time they are embedded in the organisational culture and have trouble seeing such problems clearly.

It is also important for the induction to include as much detail as possible about the company's products, services and production processes. Thorough background knowledge is an important foundation for generating useful and relevant ideas and innovations.

For individuals:

- If you do not receive a thorough induction, ask for a comprehensive briefing on products, services, clients and processes. Take this opportunity to look for gaps in the system that could be improved or altered. Spend some time thinking of solutions while your mind is still fresh and you are still slightly removed from the organisation's culture.

For organisations:

- Actively ask inductees to identify performance gaps in the organisation and give them the opportunity to discuss them.
- While an employee is relatively fresh to the organisation, ask for potential solutions while he or she is still slightly removed from the assumptions which pervade organisations and often stand in the way of fresh ideas.

An excuse to play more video games

VIDEO GAMES HAVE A bad reputation. People tend to associate them with increased aggression, childhood obesity and slothfulness. Jason used to be a bit addicted to video games. If his wife didn't object so much, he would still happily spend all his spare time playing games. However, the idea of having a video game console in the workplace would probably seem quite ridiculous to most managers.

So what do these games actually have to do with creativity? S. Shyam Sundar from Penn State University decided to research this question, (perhaps with the hope of finding results that would support his request for a gaming console for the department's staff room?)

Sundar and his colleagues set up a study that involved participants playing the game Dance Dance Revolution, following which they had to test their creative abilities. Participants' mood states were also measured.

The researchers found that playing a video game increased people's energy levels and made them feel happy, leading to increased performance on the creative problem-solving task. Specifically, the energising and entertaining effects of video games make us happy (so long as we are not on a losing streak) and contribute to boosting our creativity.

It is important to note that when it comes to increasing creativity, the type of video game can make a difference. Video games that don't have an arousing or energising effect on the player won't be that helpful in driving creativity. That said, the majority of video games energise players.

In addition, it is also important that the video game is fun, and thus makes the player feel happy. In contrast, if the game just makes the player feel a bit down or frustrated, then the creativity-inducing effects of the game won't be so pronounced. Likewise, all you need is some short spurts of gaming, as opposed to twelve-hour marathons.

For individuals:

- Bring your Gameboy or Xbox into the office and use it whenever you need to get creative juices flowing.
- Ask your boss for a video game console for the team to use when they need to think creatively.
- Try to limit game selection to those games that are energizing and fun to play.

For organisations:

- Have a video game area that staff members can use when they need to think creatively.
- Before meetings or workshops that require creative thought, give staff members ten minutes to play in the gaming area.

If creativity was
a brand…

COMPUTER USERS TEND TO classify themselves
as either a Mac or PC person. Certainly, around
Emma's office, the Mac users love and value their gear
and the PC users treat their computer as a piece of
functional furniture.

But what do computers, and more specifically,
computer makers Apple and IBM, have to do with
creativity? Sure, some of us might remember Apple's
'Think Different' campaigns from the 1990s, but did
anyone really take this literally?

Professor Gavan Fitzsimons from Duke University
and a couple of his colleagues were interested in
whether these two famous brands — one famous
for thinking differently, and the other for providing
plain beige box computers — would have on people's
ability to think creatively.

The researchers set up a study to examine
whether exposure to either of these brand's logos
would impact creative thinking behaviour. In one

study they conducted, participants were exposed to either the Apple or IBM logo. They were then asked to generate as many uses as they could think of for a brick.

The researchers found that individuals who were exposed to the Apple logo performed significantly better on the idea generation task than did the IBM people. Specifically, they generated more unusual uses for the brick, and overall, these uses were judged as being more creative compared to the IBM group's uses.

The researchers explained that because the majority of people associate Apple with creativity and being different from the norm, seeing the Apple logo can trigger these types of thoughts. This then leads to a significant increase in creative behaviour.

As stated, people have different preferences. If you prefer IBM, you can still make use of the research findings by simply posting a creative symbol near your computer that you favour.

For individuals:

- Think about brands that you associate with creativity and stick their logos (or products) up on the walls or on your desk.

For organisations:

- Deck out meeting rooms and office walls in posters of brands that you associate with creativity and innovation.

Working up a sweat

W E ALL KNOW THAT GOING to the gym makes you fit, as long as you don't overcompensate with ice cream and chocolate. Fred tries to visit his local gym at least three times a week to help him feel less guilty about all the beer he drinks every Friday night.

Recent studies have also told us that physical exercise helps us stay more alert and energetic mentally. But what effect does exercise have on creative juices?

David Blanchette and his colleagues at Rhode Island College examined this issue. They divided their research participants into three groups. Group 1 did no exercise prior to completing a creativity task. Group 2 completed thirty minutes of aerobic exercise, such as walking, bike riding, swimming or running, and immediately completed a creativity task. The final group also participated in thirty minutes of aerobic exercise, but had to wait two hours before completing the creativity task.

The researchers found that Groups 2 and 3 performed significantly better on the creativity task than the no-exercise group. They concluded that aerobic exercise enhances creativity and the positive effects are enduring; they last at least up to two hours afterward.

While I don't conduct step aerobics classes at the start of my idea generation workshops, I try to get people to stand up when they generate ideas. When people stand and move around, just as when they exercise, more blood and oxygen flows to the brain, which increases creativity.

For individuals:

- Go to the gym before work or during lunch.
- Run a mini dance class before meetings and workshops that require creativity.

For organisations:

- Consider investing in a company gym, even if it's just a meeting room with some exercise bikes and treadmills.
- Implement an employee health program where employees get points for the amount of exercise they do.

Catch me if you can

Y OU MIGHT KNOW YOUR ABCs, but do you know your three Bs of creativity? And no, none of them is beer. The three Bs of creativity are bed, bath and bus. These are the three places where the best ideas spring to mind: while we are in bed about to go to sleep or waking up in the middle of the night; when we are in the bath, shower or toilet; and when we are travelling on public transport or in the car. Unfortunately, these are also some of the best places to forget our ideas.

For Amy, her best ideas come to her when she is trying to get to sleep. But because she's so sleepy, she normally forgets these ideas come morning.

Even if you don't believe you're creative, new ideas form in your mind every hour of the day. One major difference between so-called creative people and 'non-creative' people is that the 'creatives' have learned how to pay attention and record ideas as they are formed.

Three things impede our ability to remember ideas. The first is that we overestimate our capacity to remember things. Whenever Fred dreams up a new password for his computer, he is convinced that he will remember it. However, when it's time to log in again, it has slipped his mind.

The second reason is called the 'specificity effect'. It states that we recall ideas best in the place we originally thought about them. For example, if you thought of a great idea in the shower, you should probably go and have another shower to remember it. This is one of the reasons people suggest we retrace our steps when we lose our keys. And sure enough, by doing this, we can often find them.

The third reason is that we tend to generate many ideas when we are in a musing state of mind, a state like daydreaming. However, this state of mind is not very good for laying down memory traces, so most thoughts we have in this state are not easily recalled.

Having systems in place to record ideas that enter your mind, such as a notebook or Dictaphone, is an excellent way of increasing your creative thinking output. Many well-known creative types use this approach.

Salvador Dali used to get his ideas from being in a semi-sleep state. He would hold a spoon in his hand, directly above a metal pan. When he began to drift off, the noise of the spoon hitting the pan would wake him and he would record the image he had seen in his half-asleep state.

Otto Loewi struggled for years with a problem in cell biology. One night, he dreamed a solution. He awoke, and in the dark, scribbled down his idea. Come morning, he could not read his scribbles. Clearly he was blessed, as the next night he had the same dream. Rather than take any chances, he got dressed and rushed to the lab. The work he started that night won him the Nobel Prize for Medicine in 1936.

Fred Lebow, founder of the New York City Marathon, had a novel way of recording ideas he had while on a run. Whenever a great idea came to him during a run, he'd grab a twig and scratch it into the dirt at Central Park. Later he would go back to recover his notes.

For individuals:

- Always carry around a notepad and pen, or some type of device to record your ideas. I carry around a custom-made notepad with a built-in pen so I can catch all ideas that come into my mind, no matter where I am.
- If you take up this challenge for at least a week, by the end of the week, you are likely to have a great stack of ideas.

For organisations:

- Give all employees idea-capturing notepads to take with them wherever they are. Instruct them to write down any ideas that enter their heads.
- For larger scale idea-generation sessions, brief participants on the problem a week before and give them a notepad to write down any thoughts or ideas relating to the problem. This gives the problem a chance to incubate in people's minds and will make sure you start off your idea-generation sessions with a large number of ideas already on the table.

Take the creativity challenge

NOW THAT YOU'VE REACHED the end of this book, your brain should be overflowing with practical yet simple ways in which you can immediately start to increase your own creative thinking and that of your workplace.

After finishing a book, many people feel excited about the ideas, but after a week, they forget all the knowledge they soaked up and go on with life as usual. To overcome this problem, I have a small challenge for you to ensure you get as much as possible out of what you've learned.

Every Monday morning, I want you to pick a chapter in this book and implement one of the practical tips at some stage during the week. As you have probably noticed, many of the tips can be implemented within a matter of minutes, or can involve slightly altering how you conduct a group meeting or workshop.

If you can maintain this challenge for a year (with a couple of weeks holiday), you will have implemented all fifty techniques and you will see a huge improvement in your ability to think more creatively.

Good luck on your creative thinking journey and may the rest of your year be filled with thousands of great ideas.

Acknowledgements

FIRST, THANK YOU TO ALL the psychologists and researchers who have dedicated many months (and in most cases many years) to trying to further our understanding of this phenomenon called creativity. If it weren't for your hard work and amazing results, there would be no book.

Thank you to my clients and to the people who have been audience members and participants in my presentations and workshops. You have been a huge part of my journey into the land of creativity and innovation over the last few years. Thank you for your warmth, your kind words, your open-mindedness and your enthusiasm — it has made the journey immensely richer.

Thank you to my editor Josh Mehlman, to the incredibly talented onecrazydiamond, and to savvy and smart Hooters at Hootville Communications who overflow with great ideas.

A big thank you to some of the amazing people who I am lucky enough to be surrounded by in my life, including Simon Moss, Tash Pincus, Krissie Hayes, Monique Harris, Sean Fabri — each one of you never fails to inspire me when I am in your presence. Thank you to my fellow co-founders of the Curiosity Shop, for being constant reminders and inspirers of the importance of staying curious. And thank you to Jen Stumbles and Liz Wise, who as always, were brilliant to bounce around ideas with when I became sick of talking to the wall.

A massive thank you to my writer/psychologist mother, Doris, whose creativity has greatly inspired me during my life to take risks and challenge conventions, and to my technical guru father, Martin, for his great computer advice, patience and his ability to fix anything. And to both of them for their love and unfaltering support.

Finally, thank you to my partner Shannon Dolan, for keeping me sane while trying to write a book and run a company at the same time, for loving me despite my often crazy schedule, for being so generous with so many things, and for sharing your creativity and curiosity for life with me.

Bibliography

1. **Have you warmed up your brain?**
    Forster, J., Friedman, R. S., Butterbach, E. B., &
    Sassenberg, K. (2005). Automatic effects of
    deviancy cues on creative cognition. *European
    Journal of Social Psychology, 35,* 345–359.
    Clapham, M. M. (2001). The effects of affect
    manipulation and information exposure on
    divergent thinking. *Creativity Research Journal,
    13,* 335–350.

2. **Don't worry, be happy**
    Amabile, T. M., Barsade, S. G., Mueller, J. S., & Staw,
    B. M. (2005). Affect and Creativity at Work.
    Administrative Science Quarterly, 50, 367–403.
    Gasper, K. (2004). Permission to Seek Freely? The
    Effect of Happy and Sad Moods on Generating
    Old and New Ideas. *Creativity Research Journal,
    16,* 215–229.
    Miron, E., Erez, M., & Naveh, E. (2004). Do personal
    characteristics and cultural values that promote
    innovation, quality, and efficiency compete or

complement each other? *Journal of Organizational Behavior, 25,* 175–199.

Phillips, L. H., Bull, R., Ewan, A., & Fraser, L. (2002). Positive mood and executive function: Evidence from Stroop and fluency tasks. *Emotion, 2,* 12–22.

3. **Straitjackets can be good**
   Pike, C. (2002). Exploring the conceptual space of LEGO™: Teaching and learning the psychology of creativity. *Psychology Learning and Teaching, 2,* 87–94.

4. **Bring on the newbies**
   Choi, H., & Thompson, L. (2005). Old wine in a new bottle: Impact of membership change on group creativity. *Organizational Behavior and Human Decision Processes, 98,* 121–132.

5. **Broad horizons**
   Clapham, M. M. (2001). The effects of affect manipulation and information exposure on divergent thinking. *Creativity Research Journal, 13,* 335–350.
   Shipton, H., West, M., Dawson, J., Patterson, M., & Birdi, K. (2006). Human resource management as a predictor of innovation. *Human Resource Management Journal, 16,* 3–27.

6. **Warm me up**
   McCoy, J. M., & Evans, G. W. (2002). The potential role of the physical environment in fostering creativity. *Creativity Research Journal, 14,* 409–426.

7. **Natural goodness**
   McCoy, J. M., & Evans, G. W. (2002). The potential role of the physical environment in fostering creativity. *Creativity Research Journal, 14,* 409–426.

8. **When less is less**
   McCoy, J. M., & Evans, G. W. (2002). The potential role of the physical environment in fostering creativity. *Creativity Research Journal, 14,* 409–426.

9. **Water-cooler creativity**
   McCoy, J. M., & Evans, G. W. (2002). The potential role of the physical environment in fostering creativity. *Creativity Research Journal, 14,* 409–426.

10. **Breaking the rules**
    Forster, J., Friedman, R. S., Butterbach, E. B., & Sassenberg, K. (2005). Automatic effects of deviancy cues on creative cognition. *European Journal of Social Psychology, 35,* 345–359.

11. **Up for a challenge**
    Amabile, T. M., Conti, R., Coon, H., Lazenby, J., & Herron, M. (1996). Assessing the work environment for creativity. *Academy of Management Journal, 39,* 1154–1184.

12. **Joining the dots**
    Clapham, M. M. (2001). The effects of affect manipulation and information exposure on divergent thinking. *Creativity Research Journal, 13,* 335–350.

13. **I don't want your money, honey**
    Amabile, T. M. (1998). How to Kill Creativity. *Harvard Business Review, 76,* 76–87.

14. **A pat on the back**
    Amabile, T. M. (1998). How to Kill Creativity. *Harvard Business Review, 76,* 76–87.

15. Your CV looks great, but can you think?

Poundstone, W. (2003). *How Would You Move Mount Fuji? Microsoft's Cult of the Puzzle — How the World's Smartest Company Selects the Most Creative Thinkers.* Little, Brown and Company: New York.

16. Don't box me in

Jahoda, G. (1954). A note on Ashanti names and their relationship to personality. *British Journal of Psychology, 45,* 192–195.

Jaussi, K. S., Randel, A. E., & Dionne, S. D. (2007). I am, I think I can, and I do: The role of personal identity, self-efficacy, and cross-application of experiences in creativity at work. *Creativity Research Journal, 19,* 247–258.

17. Why everyone can be a 'creative type'

Jaussi, K. S., Randel, A. E., & Dionne, S. D. (2007). I am, I think I can, and I do: The role of personal identity, self-efficacy, and cross-application of experiences in creativity at work. *Creativity Research Journal, 19,* 247–258.

18. One of a kind

Goncalo, J. A., & Staw, B. M. (2006). Individualism–collectivism and group creativity. *Organizational Behavior and Human Decision Processes, 100,* 96–109.

Lee, A. Y., Aaker, J. L., & Gardner, W. L. (200). The pleasures and pains of distinct self-construals: The role of interdependence in regulatory focus. *Journal of Personality and Social Psychology, 78,* 1122–1134.

19. Why facilitation should be mandatory

Goncalo, J. A., & Staw, B. M. (2006). Individualism–collectivism and group creativity. *Organizational*

Behavior and Human Decision Processes, 100,
96–109.

20. **Bigger isn't always better**
Hunter, S. T., Bedell, K. E., & Mumford, M. D.
(2007). Climate for creativity: A quantitative
review. *Creativity Research Journal, 19,* 69–90.

21. **Try to get along, but not too well**
Hunter, S. T., Bedell, K. E., & Mumford, M. D.
(2007). Climate for creativity: A quantitative
review. *Creativity Research Journal, 19,* 69–90.

22. **Fast-tracking intimacy**
Jaussi, K. S., & Dionne, S. D. (2003). Leading for
creativity: The role of unconventional leader
behavior. *Leadership Quarterly, 14,* 475–498.

23. **When a hot date isn't just a pretty face**
Griskevicius, V., Cialdini, R. B., & Kenrick, D.
T. (2006). Peacocks, Picasso, and parental
investment: The effects of romantic motives
on creativity. *Journal of Personality and Social
Psychology, 91,* 63–76.

24. **Dastardly deadlines**
Amabile, T. M., Conti, R., Coon, H., Lazenby,
J., & Herron, M. (1996). Assessing the
work environment for creativity. *Academy of
Management Journal, 39,* 1154–1184.

25. **Chill out**
Baumann, N. & Kuhl, J. (2002). Intuition, affect, and
personality: Unconscious coherence judgements
and self-regulation of negative affect. *Journal of
Personality and Social Psychology, 83,* 1213–1223.

26. **Mixed emotions**
Fong, C. T. (2006). The effects of emotional ambivalence on creativity. *Academy of Management Journal, 49,* 1016–1030.

27. **Brains also need support**
Amabile, T. M., Conti, R., Coon, H., Lazenby, J., & Herron, M. (1996). Assessing the work environment for creativity. *Academy of Management Journal, 39,* 1154–1184.

28. **Lead the way**
Jung, D. I., Chow, C., & Wu, A. (2003). The role of transformational leadership in enhancing organizational innovation: Hypotheses and some preliminary findings. *The Leadership Quarterly, 14,* 525–544.

29. **Sleep on it**
Dijksterhuis, A. (2004). Think Different: The Merits of Unconscious Thought in Preference Development and Decision Making. *Journal of Personality and Social Psychology, 87,* 586–598.
Dijksterhuis, A. & Nordgren, L. F. (2006). A Theory of Unconscious Thought. *Perspectives on Psychological Science, 1,* 95–109.
Dijksterhuis, A. & van Olden, Z. (2006). On the benefits of thinking unconsciously: Unconscious thought can increase post-choice satisfaction. *Journal of Experimental Social Psychology, 42,* 627–631.

30. **Sorry to interrupt you, but…**
Okhuysen, G. A. (2001). Structuring change: Familiarity and formal interventions in problem-solving groups. *Academy of Management Journal, 44,* 794–808.

31. **Rubbish in, rubbish out**
Ismail, M. (2005). Creative climate and learning organization factors: Their contribution towards innovation. *Leadership & Organization Development Journal, 26,* 639–654.

32. **Taking off the blinkers**
Friedman, R. S., Fishbach, A., Forster, J., & Werth, L. (2003). Attentional priming effects on creativity. *Creativity Research Journal, 15,* 277–286.

33. **Brainstorming is bollocks**
Epstein, R. (1996). Capturing creativity. *Psychology Today, Jul/Aug.*
Stroebe, W., & Nijstad, B. A. (2004). Why brainstorming in groups impairs creativity: A cognitive theory of productivity losses in brainstorming groups. *Psychologische Rundschau, 55,* 2–10.

34. **Why left can be right**
Baumann, N., Kuhl, J., & Kazen, M. (2005). Left-hemispheric activation and self-infiltration: Testing a neuropsychological model of internalization. *Motivation and Emotion, 29,* 135–163.

35. **I like you, but can I trust you?**
Clegg, C., Unsworth, K., Epitropaki, O., & Parker, G. (2002). Implicating trust in the innovation process. *Journal of Occupational and Organizational Psychology, 75,* 409–422.

36. **Don't try to beat 'em; join 'em**
Amabile, T. M. (1998). How to Kill Creativity. *Harvard Business Review, 76,* 76–87.

37. **Down with downsizing**
    Amabile, T. M. & Conti, R. (1999). Changes in the work environment for creativity during downsizing. *Academy of Management Journal, 42,* 630–640.

38. **Stereotyping can be good**
    Seibt, B., & Forster, J. (2004). Stereotype threat and performance: How self-stereotypes influence processing by inducing regulatory foci. *Journal of Personality and Social Psychology, 87,* 38–56.

39. **I did it my way**
    Amabile, T. M., Conti, R., Coon, H., Lazenby, J., & Herron, M. (1996). Assessing the work environment for creativity. *Academy of Management Journal, 39,* 1154–1184.
    Goncalo, J. A. (2004). Past success and convergent thinking in groups: The role of group-focused attributions. *European Journal of Social Psychology, 34,* 385–395.
    Levesque, C., & Pelletier, L. G. (2003). On the investigation of primed and chronic autonomous and heteronomous motivation orientation. *Personality and Social Psychology Bulletin, 29,* 1570–1584.
    Ramamoorthy, N., Flood, P. C., Slattery, T., & Sardessai, R. (2005). Determinants of Innovative Work Behaviour: Development and Test of an Integrated Model. *Creativity and Innovation Management, 14,* 142–150.

40. **Cut up your tie**
    Morand, D. A. (1995). The role of behavioral formality and informality in the enactment of bureaucratic versus organic organizations. *Academy of Management Review, 20,* 831–872.

41. Why you shouldn't want it to be a team effort
Goncalo, J. A. (2004). Past success and convergent thinking in groups: The role of group-focused attributions. *European Journal of Social Psychology, 34,* 385–395.

42. Talking in the abstract
Ward, T. B., Patterson, M. J., & Sifonis, C. M. (2004). The role of specificity and abstraction in creative idea generation. *Creativity Research Journal, 16,* 1–9.

43. Forward to the future
Forster, J., Friedman, R. S., & Liberman, N. (2004). Temporal construal effects on abstract and concrete thinking: Consequences for insight and creative cognition. *Journal of Personality and Social Psychology, 87,* 177–189.

Friedman, R. S., & Forster, J. (2001). The effects of promotion and prevention cues on creativity. *Journal of Personality and Social Psychology, 87,* 177–189.

Yadav, M. S., Prabhu, J. C., & Chandy, R. K. (2007). Managing the Future: CEO Attention and *Innovation Outcomes. Journal of Marketing, 71,* 84–101.

44. Scrap the detail
Ruscio, A. M., & Amabile, T. M. (1999). Effects of instructional style on problem-solving creativity. *Creativity Research Journal, 12,* 251–266.

45. I think therefore I can
Jaussi, K. S., Randel, A. E., & Dionne, S. D. (2007). I am, I think I can, and I do: The role of personal identity, self-efficacy, and cross-application of experiences in creativity at work. *Creativity Research Journal, 19,* 247–258.

46. Inductrination
   Shipton, H., West, M., Dawson, J., Patterson, M., & Birdi, K. (2006). Human resource management as a predictor of innovation. *Human Resource Management Journal, 16,* 3–27.

47. An excuse to play video games
   Sundar, S. S., & Hutton, E. (2008). Can Video Games Enhance Creativity? An Experimental Investigation of Emotion Generated by Dance Dance Revolution. 58th annual conference of the International Communication Association, Montreal.

48. If creativity was a brand...
   Fitzsimons, G. M., Chartrand, T. L., & Fitzsimons, G. J. (2008). Automatic Effects of Brand Exposure on Motivated Behavior: How Apple Makes You "Think Different". *Journal of Consumer Research, 35,* 21–35.

49. Working up a sweat
   Blanchette, D. M., Ramocki, S. P., O'Del, J. N., & Casey, M. S. (2005). Aerobic exercise and creative potential: Immediate and residual effects. *Creativity Research Journal, 17,* 257–264.

50. Catch me if you can
   Baddeley, A. (1999). *Essentials of Human Memory.* Taylor & Francis: London.

Index

About the author

D<small>R. AMANTHA IMBER</small> is the founder of Inventium, an international creativity and innovation company. Amantha has a Doctorate in Organisational Psychology, which means that aside from being able to read minds better than most people, she brings a scientific yet highly practical approach to the field of creativity and innovation.

Through Inventium, Amantha has worked with C-Level executives through to university graduates, and has clients across Australia, the United States, the United Kingdom, New Zealand, Africa, and Europe. Her clients include LEGO, Kimbery-Clark, Ogilvy + Mather, BP, Deloitte, OMD, Qantas, Vodafone, and Fosters.

Amantha has written extensively on the subjects of creativity and innovation, and her words can be read in *Fast Thinking, Marketing Magazine, Contagious, Human Capital Magazine, Motivation Magazine, Australian Anthill, Marketing Profs, B&T Weekly, International Journal of Selection and*

Assessment, and *Educational and Psychological Measurement and Evaluation.*

Amantha is an in-demand speaker at innovation conferences and events all around the world and has presented to thousands of people about how they can turbo-charge their ability to think creatively.

Amantha had an international record deal for her debut album 'Like Samantha without the S', prays to the God of Kevin Spacey, and used to be freakishly good at table tennis.

Want to know more?

Go to *www.thecreativityformula.com* and
subscribe to Amantha's free e-newsletter that has
creativity-inducing tidbits in every issue.